EVERYTHING THE CAT LOVER WANTS TO KNOW ABOUT . . .

- SELECTING A BREED—The differences between Siamese, Persian, Abyssinian, the American Shorthair, and other cats are emotional as well as physical. Which one is best for you?

- FEEDING—What should you feed your cat, how much, and how often? What about water, vitamins and minerals? Should cats eat dogfood and babyfood? There are many things to know about the healthiest diet for your cat.

- ENVIRONMENT—When should a cat be allowed outside the house? When is a walk-in cage a necessity? Do indoor cats need sun and an outdoors view? Where should breeding take place? It is up to you to make your cat's home a happy one.

- THE KILLER DISEASE—Panleukopenia. What is it and when does it strike? How can you protect your cat against this dread illness?

- KITTENS—How to protect them before birth. How and when to help with the delivery. When to install a cattery. How to humor mama cat. This can be the cat person's most satisfying experience . . . and biggest responsibility.

- AND MUCH, MUCH MORE—About grooming, spaying, de-clawing, litter boxes, children, strays, immunization—EVERYTHING THE CAT OWNER NEEDS TO KNOW!

A NOTE TO OUR READERS:

As a general rule, your cat should not have anything attached around its neck as collars and ribbons may cause fatal accidents. The collar or bow could get caught on something and the cat could strangle himself trying to get free. The bow around the neck of the kitten on our cover was worn only for photographic purposes.

If it is necessary for you to attach an item around your cat's neck—for identification, for example, if you live in suburban or rural areas—be sure to use only collars made with an elastic safety section.

HANDBOOK FOR
CAT PEOPLE

Celia Heriot

AWARD BOOKS
NEW YORK

TANDEM BOOKS
LONDON

HOW TO BECOME A SUPPORTING MEMBER OF PET PRIDE

The struggle to improve the status of our nation's cats is of great importance and cannot be set aside any longer. PET PRIDE's funds go toward the humane control of the cat over-population and help provide medical attention for thousands of injured, abandoned and homeless cats.

In addition, PET PRIDE is active in spreading helpful information on the proper ways to care for cats and provide them with a healthful, clean, attractive environment. PET PRIDE's ultimate goal is to build as many model shelters as are needed for homeless cats throughout the country.

PET PRIDE is a non-profit organization wholly dependent on the contributions of cat people. For $7.00 a year you can become a supporting member of PET PRIDE. Anything else you can afford to send will be most gratefully appreciated. All contributions are of course tax-deductible.

Please clip and mail this application today

PET PRIDE
Pacific Palisades,
California 90272

(213) 459-1703

I support PET PRIDE's aims and wish to become a member. Enclosed is my contribution of $——————————(I understand that a minimum of $7.00 entitles me to one year's membership).

Name———————————————————————————

Address—————————————————————————

City————————————State————Zip—————

CONTENTS

PREFACE

For decades cats have been shamefully neglected, improperly if not cruely treated and carelessly handled. These intelligent, sensitive, companionable animals count on us for decent care. Whether or not they get it depends on the enthusiasm, knowledge and ethics of their owners.

People must be made aware of the dreadful fate that millions of cats across the country now face. Educational centers, model clinics and properly run shelters are needed. Shows, seminars, exhibitions and fund-raising benefits —all these will help. Step by step, the layman must be taught to protect and love the cat, to become a true Cat Person. I sincerely hope this book will help attain that end.

Members of the Cat Fanciers Association, the official registering and standard-setting organization in this country, account for only perhaps a quarter of a million of this country's cats. All the same, because of their expert knowledge and intense interest in cats, they are uniquely qualified to act as educators of the general cat owner.

Many chapters in this book demanded specialized knowledge, and they have been written by those whose first-hand experience best fits them to speak. I give you therefore not only my own thoughts and the results of my research, but the contributions of many who have outstanding insight into the life of cats.

1

Chapter 1

HERE'S TO THE CAT

Cats are lucky—how often have we heard someone say that as he looks at a contented, purring cat? Maybe these people think cats are lucky because they don't have to work for their bed and board like as humans do. Perhaps they mean cats are lucky because they don't worry and stew as much as people do—they seem to have a calmer, saner view of things.

But when someone says, "Cats are lucky," he is only partly right. Some cats are lucky—those owned by devoted Cat People. But other cats—millions and millions of them—aren't so lucky. There are unlucky registered and purebred cats whose owners are out-and-out cruel in their negligence. Some cats are housed in small cages day in and day out, to suffer lonely boredom with no exercise whatever. Some are kept in unfinished garages and basements among dirty litter pans which make a repulsive, ill-smelling hell on earth.

And then there are the unlucky homeless cats—roving strays, abandoned, thirsty, starving, disease-ridden.

Who is doing anything to help these millions of unlucky cats? Pet Pride is one of the organizations trying to deal systematically with this serious problem. Pet Pride is a humane, educational institution. Many think of Pet Pride

as a philosophy. Pet Pride people have developed a philosophical attitude toward the great cause of helping cats. It is they who are doing the missionary work of solving many serious cat problems.

Every Pet Pride member pledges himself to help promote and maintain ideal living conditions for his cats, to hold rigid standards of cat care conducive to the health, beauty and happiness of these dependent animals, and to encourage a spirit of cooperation, helpfulness, loyalty and honor among the members of the Cat Fancy and all other pet owners.

Pet Pride tries to educate the public about cats with literature published in magazines, distributed at shows and other public meetings and in the veterinarians's office. They also carry on an enormous correspondence with cat owners who are seeking information, other than medical, about their cats.

Pet Pride is unusual among humane organizations in that it began with and includes many members of the Cat Fancy—that is, those people involved with purebred cats. In this lies the organization's strength, for although the number of cats in the Fancy includes only a small percent-

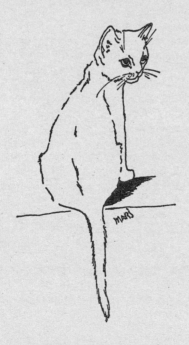

age of the cats in the world, their owners know more about cats than anyone.

Again, the Fancy is organized. It is willing and anxious to share available educational materials. It is qualified to help the pet owner and to work for the passage of humane laws. The great majority of pet owners do not communicate with each other or exchange information about their pets. The show can be a meeting place of the pet owner, the Fancy cat owner, and the humane worker. Each has much to give the other.

The greater part of Pet Pride's resources are spent not on the purebred but on the mixed-breed cat. The owners of mixed-breed cats are unorganized and many of them allow their cats to run loose. These cats are killed in traffic in great numbers. If picked up and placed in a public shelter, they are either sent to the laboratory for experimental purposes or euthanized.

Although Pet Pride people are not interested solely in purebred cats, they do wish to keep the different breeds alive, distinct and healthy. They feel that purebred cats help capture public interest in all cats, as well as maintain interesting and beautiful cat qualities which are specific to certain breeds.

Pet Pride's hope is that as it continues to work on the proper care of cats, promotes the welfare of cats, stimulates interest in cat status, and inspires the potential benefactor to invest in cats, their lives will improve.

The main hope of the cat today is the interested Cat Person, whether or not he belongs to an organization dedicated to helping cats. Just what is a Cat Person?

A Cat Person can imagine himself in the cat's place.

A Cat Person has a sincere feeling of compassion for all animals.

A Cat Person is open-minded and willing to accept basic facts on care.

A Cat Person is generous with time and money spent on the cat.

A Cat Person will listen to his veterinarian.

A Cat Person is responsible for the good life of all kittens he causes to be brought into this world.

A Cat Person has respect for all cats, not just one particular breed, or one particular group.

A Cat Person will protect his cat from harm, loneliness and disease.

A Cat Person is proud of his cats.

If Cat People work together, they cannot help but succeed in making life more comfortable for all cats.

Part I

BREEDS OF CATS

Chapter 2

WHY NOT OWN A SIAMESE?

I have an adolescent Siamese on my lap, trying to convince me that it would be nicer to hold him than to type. Don't buy a Siamese unless you can give him a great deal of love, unless you have a keen sense of humor, unless you enjoy an active, mischievous cat.

A Siamese is svelte, regal in appearance. When running and playing, he is a streak of lightning, graceful as a panther. He thinks up tricks to play on you, he brings you gifts. He sits on your lap and stares lovingly into your eyes, trying to communicate. When hungry, he has been known to rummage in the trash, if he can get at it, for a carton that contained his food, and then to bring it to you in his teeth to show you what he wants.

Siamese cats are marvelous travelers by air, sea or land. They can be trained to walk on a leash and to use the toilet, which is wonderful because it eliminates the sandbox. The other morning I trained a kitten to retrieve a paper rolled into a ball while I was having coffee.

The best way to purchase a kitten is to attend a cat show and take the names and addresses of Siamese owners and breeders from the catalog; or try the yellow pages under "Catteries." Often a veterinarian can refer you to a reputable breeder. Pet stores sometimes keep a local list-

ing. If there is a branch of Pet Pride in your city, it has a directory of breeders.

Don't be afraid to pay for a good kitten. The old adage holds true. You get what you pay for. Divide the cost by fifteen, which is the number of years a cat can be expected to live with good care, and you will find that you are paying three to four dollars a year for a wonderful companion. A good pet Siamese should cost about fifty dollars and should be approximately three months old. Many people want the youngest kitten they can find. This is a sad mistake. A kitten of eight weeks is too young to be taken from his mother and family. He will be frightened in a new environment and consequently won't eat for a day or so. A kitten that young can be in serious trouble if he goes without food that long. He can die. Beware of breeders who sell kittens six to eight weeks old. An older kitten has a reserve to fall back on while he is making the difficult adjustment to a new home, new food and strange people.

Any kitten should have had his permanent panleukopenia shot before he is sold. He should not have any trace of watery eyes or runny nose. The breeder should advise you on the kitten's diet and offer to answer any questions you may want to ask after the sale. A reputable breeder is definitely interested in the kitten's transition to his new home.

Unfortunately, some people offer for sale litters sired by the male down the street. They think big money can be made by selling kittens. These people sell kits for five to ten dollars and never want to see you or the kitten again. If the kit dies, that's tough.

It will pay you to take the time to find a reputable breeder. You may want to purchase a pet rather than a pedigree, but it's nice to know that the ancestors of your loved one were registered cats from good lines.

A Siamese should always, without exception, have blue eyes. The coats come in varying colors:

Seal points—Almost black points (face, legs, ears, tail). Body is beige or fawn color.

Blue points—Blue-gray points. Body sparkling bluish white.

Chocolate points—Milk-chocolate color points. Body cream color. Paw leather cinnamon pink.

Lilac (frost) points—Points should be a light silvery blue with a slight rosiness showing through the ears. Body glacial white. Paw leather salmon pink. Blood tones to show through the nose leather.

Occasionally you will find Siamese with kinks in their tails and crossed eyes. These do not detract from a cat's qualities as a pet, although he would be penalized for these characteristics if he were shown.

Your Siamese will always be at the door to greet you upon your arrival home, ready to play or to talk over the day's happenings. Yes, they do talk. After you have lived with them for a while, you will understand what they are saying. When you speak to them, they will answer you.

Siamese are good children's pets. The child must be taught to treat the cat with gentleness, of course.

Siamese and dogs can become great buddies. And two Siamese are more fun than one. I like to call them a community cat. They love company. They will entertain themselves, you and your friends with their antics and they will be company for each other when you are away. However, if you have only one, by all means have him. If you must be away all day, the cat will curl up and sleep the hours away and be ready to visit and play when you arrive home.

Some beliefs I would like to explode:

"Siamese are mean." Only someone who knows nothing about them could possibly say this. You will never believe

their capacity for love until you own one. The sad exceptions that have given the breed a bad name are those who have been mistreated and have defensively fought back. If a cat scratches, it is usually because he has been surprised and frightened or mistreated.

"They are so loud!" Permit me to say that only an unhappy Siamese is loud. If your cat is content, he will sleep while you are away. When you are home he will talk to you or curl up in your lap or sing you a lovely song.

"Siamese are destructive." The factor of intelligence comes up again. Siamese are like children and must be disciplined, especially during the first year of life. If you are firm and consistent with "no" and a light tap with a newspaper, the cat soon learns that what he is doing is displeasing you and he will stop—unless he wants to attract your attention and has no alternative except to break a rule. A scratching pole or tree for exercise,

stretching and climbing, can be covered in your own dec-orator colors. The proud cat who owns one of these will leave the furniture and carpet alone. Siamese can be taught to stay off tables and counters if you are firm and consistent about it.

These cats are jealous, protective, independent. You have to be on your toes to figure how their minds work and to keep ahead of them. They are a never-ending source of humor and enjoyment. You really haven't lived until you've been owned by a Siamese.

Marge Naples

Chapter 3

PERSIANS—THE FLOWER CHILDREN

Persians, with their long flowing coats and delicate pansylike faces, are surely the flower children of the Cat Fancy. They are gentle, peace-loving animals who seem to live by the Chinese philosophy of Taoism, which teaches that everything in the universe is designed to move in an ordered and harmonic way.

Their calm dispositions and natural beauty make them greatly sought after as companions for both adults and children. They are extremely adaptable, managing equally well in an apartment or a home with secluded garden. They will spend long hours draped in a favorite position,

adding beauty to their surroundings in much the same way as an *objet d'art*.

They come in a rainbow of colors, from pristine white to exotic jungle tints. The whites are divided into three different color classes. Some have blue eyes, some copper, and some have the surprising combination of one blue and one copper eye.

The massive blues have for many years exhibited the finest characteristics of the breed. They have been used to intensify the Persian "type" in almost all other colors. This magnificent cat, the apex of the breed, cannot be truly appreciated under artificial lighting. Sunlight refracts as it hits the coat, giving the color added dimensions.

The blacks, with their patent-leather lustre and blood-red eyes, and the creams with their milk-colored coats, are favorites in the show ring. The red cats, who were once one of the most popular, now appear in the shows sparsely.

The most ethereal of all Persians are the silvers. Their deep green or blue-green eyes are outlined with black, giving them the appearance of prima ballerinas. They are basically white, but the fur is tipped with black. The chinchillas, palest of the silvers, appear sparkling white. Careful scrutiny reveals gentle tipping on the face, the ruff and throughout the coat. It should extend ever so lightly on the legs. The foot leather is black, a remarkable contrast to the coat. A deep brick-red nose, which is also outlined with black, finishes this confection in much the same way as a cherry adds appeal to an ice cream sundae. The shaded silvers are much darker in tone than the chinchillas. Whereas from a distance the chinchilla appears white, the shaded is a deeper, almost gunmetal, color, under the special patina of the tipping.

The shell cameo and the shaded cameo are also basically white, but tipped with red. Their nose leather and footpads are rosy-toned and their eyes a deep copper. The shell is the paler of the two, and the red tipping gives him a delicate glow. The red-shaded burns with deeper intensity.

One of the most striking Persians is the smoke. We recognize three separate colors, the black, the blue and the red smoke. In each case the cat appears to be solid color with a white or silver frill and ear tufts. In motion, the coat will break open, giving glimpses of a startling white undercoat. The deep copper eyes are embers in their smoke setting.

Tabbies are the extroverts of the breed. They come in thirteen colors and two pattern types, classic and mackerel. The brilliantly contrasted markings can be as exotic as a jungle cat's. Often referred to as the fun cats, the tabbies are outgoing and demonstrative.

There is also a "Peke-face" Persian in both solid red and red tabby. These cats conform to the basic standard for color, but have heads that resemble the Pekinese dog. The nose should be extremely short and depressed and the face should have a decidedly wrinkled muzzle.

Females dominate among the parti-color cats. Tortoiseshell, calico and blue-cream males are totally nonexistent. The tortie is a brilliantly-colored black cat dispersed with great splotches of red and cream. A division of color on the face, known as the blaze, adds interest to this brightly colored variety. The calico, rarely encountered in the show rings, is white with areas of red, black, and cream. The blue-cream, a delightful study in pastel, is a solid blue cat patched with cream. The cream patching should extend from her toes to her tail. The muted coloring of the blue-cream is as softly lovely as the tortie is eye-catching and brilliant.

Persians are gentle. Their stable personalities are often misleading. Those who do not look beyond their surface traits refer to them as cold or unresponsive. Nothing could be further from the truth. Though conservative by nature, they are devoted pets and make tremendous "family-member" cats. Quiet and unobtrusive, they quickly establish their places in your household and your heart.

Persians have been an important part of my life since I was a child. My first purebred—a red Persian—was a present for my sixteenth birthday. I cannot imagine the agony and the ecstasy of those teenage years without Pud-

din. How many tears I cried into her lovely red coat! How often she would curl up in my lap and gently pat my face as if to say, "I'm here and I will always love you." And she did, for nineteen wonderful years.

Puddin always planned her litters to arrive when I was with her. Once when I was away at college, she fretted and fumed until I arrived home for a holiday. The instant I walked in the door she promptly climbed into her nesting box and within a few minutes triumphantly delivered her new family.

I fell in love during my senior year of college. Most girls receive their marriage proposal with a simple yes, no or maybe. I cautiously asked, "May I have my cats?"

His answer? "Honey, you can have all the cats you want!" I sometimes wonder if he regrets that promise when he can't find a catless chair to sit in.

Cats and babies? We combined the two when we brought home our first-born daughter from the hospital. The cats revealed a tremendous curiosity as to what was so interesting in the pink and white bassinet. Each in turn quietly investigated—and quickly retreated from my noisy, squirming infant. They never again showed more than a passing interest in her until she was old enough to play.

Once the baby captured our yearling male, Mickey, by the tail. I heard his frantic cries for help and his scrambling on the waxed floor over her squeals of delight. It never occurred to him to hurt her, even though he wanted desperately to be freed. Instead, he cried for me. That's the way Persians are.

A passage from the Tao Te Ching, a book on Chinese philosophy, might well be applied to these flower children of the Cat Fancy, our Persians.

"The heavens continue, and the earth endures;
   And that in them which makes them so permanent
   Is that they do not live for themselves.
   Thus it is that they can live so long."

Mrs. Frank M. (Jeanie) McPhee

Chapter 4

THE BEST OF TWO WORLDS

Each breed of cat has its admirers. Talk with those who own any purebred cat, and they will quickly point out why theirs is the most desirable. The shorthair fancier will dwell upon the convenience of having only small quantities of fine hair to worry about when cleaning the house (*all* cats will shed, of course). At a less utilitarian level, his admirer will speak of the shorthair's personality and antics. On the other side of the coin, the proponent of the longhair will stress the cloud of soft, long hair that forms a coat of outstanding beauty. The longhair fancier also brags of his cat's melodious voice, as opposed to the louder, more raucous call of many shorthairs.

For those who fancy the traits of both the shorthair and the longhair, there is an answer—the Himalayan. The Himalayan, or Colour Point Longhair as it is called in England and Europe, combines the best of both worlds.

The Himalayan results from arduous work over many years by two people. They set out to capture in one animal the body, coat and head of the Persian and the beautiful color patterns of the shorthair Siamese.

The Himalayan is a developed breed—that is to say, produced by serious cat breeders, working with the laws of genetics. Marguerita Goforth originated the breed in the United States by crossing the shorthaired Siamese with the longhaired Persian. The task took ten years of selective

breeding. At the same time, Brian A. Stirling-Webb was working independently in England. Brian and Marguerita were unaware of each other's efforts. The Stirling-Webb cats were recognized as the Colour Point Longhair, while the Goforth cats were called the Himalayan. From their pioneer work have developed the famous Himalayan cats of today.

Many ask me if they, too, can produce a Himalayan if they breed their Siamese to a Persian. The answer is *no*. Most likely, the first cross of Persian to Siamese will produce *black shorthair* kittens. If you want Himalayans, the best procedure is to purchase a Himalayan kitten. People have also asked me if they could improve their Himalayans by breeding them back to a Siamese or a Per-

sian. Again the answer is no. To outcross the original breed may take years of selective breeding to overcome unforeseen difficulties—loss of eye color, muddy coat, wrong eye shape. The serious breeder may be willing to cope with these problems, but not the average owner.

The Himalayan is affectionate and will literally wilt from lack of attention. They love being under the covers, snuggled up with their people at night. They establish their own set household rules, and will let their people know it whenever a rule is broken. Nothing is quite as ego-deflating as a Himalayan acting as if his human did not exist. Minutes to hours later, generally after coaxing and proper apologies have been tendered, the slight is forgiven and cat and owner reunited. The cat, of course, is the winner—never the other way round. As always, affection and delightful companionship are offered—if merited. No servility should be expected, only mutual respect.

The Himalayan, properly bred, needs little attention beyond an occasional combing. The texture of the coat is such that little matting occurs. Given warm, dry, clean surroundings, the Himalayan's coat will bloom year round. After having been taken outdoors—with proper supervision—his coat should be thoroughly checked for leaves or burrs.

For the longhair, diet is important. The Himalayan requires raw meat, vitamins, vegetables and his choice of special treats. Mine adore yeast tablets which go by the name of "candy" and are given every day. Chahila, grand champion and top-flight show cat that she is, demands two special treats—Canadian bacon and Cadbury's milk chocolate. The frying of the bacon produces somersaults, purrs, sitting up and extended conversation to make sure that I don't forget her. On very special occasions, a small bite of Cadbury's is licked, worried, and finally swallowed amidst rolling of eyes and actual smiles on Chahila's little face. I don't recommend candy for cats, but be prepared to have your Himalayan develop rather special tastes which become his high point reward!

The Himalayan's voice is generally well-mannered. When particularly excited, he will chat at length with you—expecting answers to his feline comments and observations. By the way, never laugh at him, only with him—any Cat Person will know the difference.

All Himalayans have deep, vivid blue eyes. Kittens can be obtained in the following coat colors:

Chocolate point—The body color is ivory. The point color (mask, ears, paws and tail) is a warm, milk-chocolate color. Nose leather and paw pads are cinnamon pink.

Seal point—The body color is an even pale fawn or cream and is warm in tone (no bluish overtones) and gradually shades to a lighter color on the stomach and chest. The points are deep seal brown. The paw pads and nose leather are also deep seal brown.

Blue point—The body is a cold, bluish white gradually shading to white on the stomach and chest. The points are blue (a lovely mist shade). Nose leather and paw pads are slate-colored.

Lilac point—The body is pristine, glacial white with no shading. The point color is a frosty gray with a pinkish undertone. Paw pads and nose leather are lavender pink.

Flame point—The body color is creamy white. The point color is a flame orange shade—devoid of bars and stripes. Nose leather and paw pads are an orange-pink tone.

Tortie point—The body is creamy white in color. The points are black with unbridled patches of red and cream. Nose leather and paw pads are predominately black with patches of pink.

These colors are recognized for championship competition. Other Himalayan colors occur but are not eligible for championship. Among these other colors are blue-cream points and lynx points. I would recommend that the Himalayan owner leave these colors to the serious breeder. Achieving recognition for such colors for championship competition may be a long and arduous process.

Recently a new color has appeared, a self chocolate Himalayan. This cat is a solid warm brown in color without points. A cat of great beauty, he is a by-product, colorwise, of selective breeding. At this time, self chocolates are extremely rare. I would predict a great future for them, even if, unlike other Himalayans, they are not a "pointed" cat. A true brown longhair has been the dream of cat fanciers for many years.

I recommend the Himalayan to all. It has the beautiful coloring we love in the Siamese and the coat and body of the Persian—the best of both possible worlds.

Will P. Thompson

Chapter 5

THE EXOTIC CATS MUST LIVE, TOO!

My wife and I share a love of animals in general and the larger cats in particular. When we married, we wanted a wild-born feline for a pet, yet one that would fit our apartment and would not be deprived for lack of an expensive run.

In one book we had read, the ocelot was described as fitting these qualifications. Before buying the cat we would love and keep for all its life and a large portion of our own, we sought information from any and all sources. We visited pet shops, talked with attendants there, visited ocelot owners and read whatever literature was available. Our research yielded several surprises, some good, but mostly bad.

The ocelot is one of the smaller species of the free-living cats. He usually weighs between twenty and forty pounds, with exceptions weighing to sixty or more. No one can predict his future stature by his appearance as a kitten. Surprisingly long for the width of his body, he measures about three feet discounting the tail, with the female approximately twenty percent smaller than the

male. The physical strength of every exotic cat is truly
exceptional.

The ocelot kitten is usually captured by hunters in
South America. When a hunter discovers a mother with
her litter of two, he kills her by clubbing, while the kittens
watch. He cannot shoot her since the bullet hole would
ruin her pelt, which he means to sell. This is the ocelot
kitten's first experience with man.

At base camp, these kittens are kept in small crates, fed
and watered only slightly. When the hunter has accumu-
lated enough pelts and kittens, he returns to the exporter's
compound. The kittens are kept, still under inhumane
and disease-spreading conditions, until the exporter has
enough kittens to ship, again in small crates to avoid high
transportation charges, to various pet shops and import-
ers.

When the kittens arrive at pet shops, they are usually mistreated both because of the operator's ignorance of the species and their needs and because of simple callousness. Some estimate that only fifty percent of the captive kittens survive. Others place the mortality rate far higher. Only ten percent will live to find a home.

We found from personal experience that pet store operators, with few exceptions, will give no guarantee on an ocelot. The speedy sale is best; otherwise, the kitten may die before the pet store operator can sell him.

The ocelot's personality is fragile. He is timid and needs much attention to reinforce his confidence and dissipate his fears. Most ocelots fear strangers. They are definitely private pets, wanting to be only with their families.

One Sunday in a local pet store we saw Tammy for the first time, cowering in the back of a large cage. A very small ocelot, at the time she weighed fourteen pounds. She was chained to the cage wall. In the cage to the left was a puma whose greatest enjoyment came from reaching into Tammy's cage and trying to grab her. While we were watching this pitiable cat, one of the attendants came along and said that this ocelot was not friendly, but that he was training her to be.

He entered the cage with gloves, grabbed the chain, and held Tammy's head to the floor while he "stroked" her with his other gloved hand. The puma, meanwhile, was still trying to grab her. At this point we bought an ocelot.

Tam had been owned before and had been brought back to the pet store when she had started to mature.

When we brought our cat home, she was so frightened that she crawled under the sofa and remained there for two weeks except to eat or to use her box, during the times when we left her alone. We have now owned Tammy for four years and she is still making progress in befriending us. It has been a long, difficult period for her, but fortunately the relationship seems to tend toward success.

This is not always the outcome with an ocelot who, like Tammy, has been owned before.

The person who buys an ocelot should, for the cat's sake, keep him whether or not he becomes a pest, an inconvenience, whether he needs expensive veterinary care, even if he never becomes a pet. Most of these cats simply do not adapt well to a second owner. To give away an exotic is to sentence him, as a rule, to a life of misery.

If an ocelot kitten is very nervous and fearful, discipline of any kind would only retard his progress toward a less troubled state. He needs to gain confidence in his owner and surroundings. On the other hand, if the kitten is obviously unafraid, disciplining by voice or by slaps with a folded newspaper would be advised.

When the kitten is first received, he must be taken to a qualified veterinarian. Here is another surprise. Most veterinarians are not qualified to diagnose and treat exotics. Many ocelots have been killed through improper handling by the veterinarian. The ocelot's nervous system is different from the domestic cat's. The ocelot is extremely sensitive to both anesthesia and tranquilizers. He may react to a tranquilizer by becoming agitated. The anesthetic dose for a domestic cat may kill an ocelot outright. His depth of unconsciousness must be constantly monitored in surgery. Most exotic owners shy away from surgical procedures such as spaying.

In other than emergency cases, the only veterinarian who should be allowed to touch an exotic is one who has studied the type and their unique health problems. Many ocelots have died of heart arrest induced by fear when being examined. The experienced doctor, when presented with this type of exotic, will vary his methods accordingly.

Most exotics need more veterinary care than the domestic cat. This may seem contradictory since they care for themselves in a jungle. In this country, however, they are exposed to new diseases for which they have no resistance.

The ocelot's worst enemy is feline enteritis, which he can catch from his domestic cousin. He must be vaccinated against this disease and must receive a booster injection every year, to insure immunity continuance. The owner of the exotic must be prepared to spend great amounts of money for veterinary care.

Speaking of expenses, the cost of the ocelot varies considerably throughout the United States. In the northeast, where we live, ocelots sell in the range of three to five hundred dollars.

Many owners have their exotics' canine teeth either removed or filed down. Neither of these procedures should be allowed. Although filing may seem harmless, it is almost impossible to do without removing all enamel. With pulp and nerve exposed, infection is sure to follow. Here again the cat must suffer needlessly and must submit to having the tooth removed to prevent the spread of infection which could easily prove fatal.

The removal of canines is dangerous on at least two counts. First, the cat must be put into deep sleep, a chancy thing with his species. Second, the ocelot's canine teeth are strongly imbedded in his skull and jawbone. In fact, the lower canines change direction inside the jaw and run parallel to it. This enables the cat to walk and climb with heavy loads in his mouth. Many, many ocelots have had their jaws broken during the defanging operation.

Owners may want their cat's canines removed because the ocelot uses his mouth frequently while playing or while trying to put a message across to his owner such as, "Hey, hurry up there, I'm hungry." The ocelot does bite frequently and at times hard. This is a natural part of his life and little if anything can be done about it. Defanging is not the answer. The ocelot can apply just about the same amount of pressure with his other teeth and any slight benefit gained is more than offset by the dangers involved. If a person wants a cat that will not bite or hurt him, he should not buy an exotic. The ocelot owner must

resign himself to the fact that he will always have black
and blue marks, bruises and bites from his cat.

Altering is seldom done to an exotic. The female,
especially, must be put deeply under anesthesia for the
operation. The main reason for altering is another of the
ocelot's less admirable characteristics. Even though, like
other cats, the ocelot is clean, using his box as does a
domestic cat, he must also periodically "stake out" his
area by spraying urine at various points. Of course these
points are inside the home. The ocelot's urine is much
more highly scented than the domestic's and, unless the
owner is careful to completely wipe up all sprays and
unless he changes the cat's litter boxes often, the home
will soon develop a very distinctive odor.

Even the most fastidious owner soon finds that a certain
amount of odor is present, but this can, at least, be kept to
a minimum. The female sprays most frequently while in
heat. If spayed, she will still spray, but not as frequently.
Also, if she is spayed, she will have less chance of
devloping cystic ovaries.

The exotic cat's personality is as varied as that of its
owners. Some are introverts, others extroverts; some are
timid, others aggressive; some friendly, others hostile.
The ocelot kitten may be immediately trusting and fear-
less, or so frightened that he will hiss, spit and try to
scratch his new owner when approached. Most ocelot
kittens—and exotic kittens in general—will have personalities somewhere between these extremes and, with a few
days of patient, gentle and understanding treatment, will
become friendly and adjusted to their new lives. The
adaptability of the young of any species is astounding.

Periodically, however, a kitten is received that does not
respond to kindness; he retains his fearful and defensive
attitudes much of his life, forming no close relationship
with anyone. A person who buys an ocelot must understand this and be ready to keep this cat, to love him even
though no love is returned, to give him the best care pos-

sible and to give him the best life that the owner can. He must not return this cat and submit him to a life of multiple ownership only to end in a zoo. I stress this because this type of cat shows up more often than most people believe and is usually returned with the abovementioned results. There is a possibility that a cat of this type will respond to his owner's kindness after one, two, or more years—but only a possibility.

Most ocelots have nervous temperaments. Any unusual movement or tone of voice will immediately awaken them from sleep. They are ever watchful and cautious, entering into new situations only after thoroughly investigating the harmful possibilities. Some are only moderately nervous while others will jump at the least unexpected sound. The more nervous cats are also fearful of quick movements and, should an owner receive a cat of this type, he will have to watch his gestures in his cat's presence. Some of the nervous kittens will become calmer as they mature, but most will not; the owner will have to protect a cat of this type for the cat's entire life from any startling move or sound.

Most ocelots grow to be friendly with their owners and, usually but not always, with the rest of the family. The ocelot enjoys rough playing. If a dog or house cat does not like children's roughhousing, he will run away and try to avoid them in the future. The ocelot kitten will return their roughness with a little extra of his own. At first this is cute. The kitten does little damage. However, as he matures, he becomes incredibly strong. Since he believes rough play is permissible, he will continue it with resulting bites and scratches for the children. At this point many people decide to give away or sell the cat, with the probable ensuing tragedy for the animal; or they decide that he has "reverted" and have him killed by a veterinarian— equally tragic.

Should an ocelot have the freedom of the house? The new kitten should be kept in a small area or at least have recourse to a small private section such as his packing box or similar enclosure. Now at his most fearful, he needs the security of four small walls. This is not the time for the entire family to gather around and pet the kitten unless he is obviously unafraid and enjoys attention. Once he becomes accustomed to his new surroundings, his area of freedom should be expanded until finally he has the run of the house or apartment.

Of course, it is not cruel to keep him temporarily in a single room if visitors are not appreciative of the exotic. Also he may be banned from one or more specific areas, such as an aquarium. However, his domestic development is certain to be stunted if he is kept in a cage for the greater part of the day or permanently confined.

The diet of the ocelot is varied and, as with other facets of his life, no rigid standards can be set. The goal to strive for, especially while the kitten is growing, is balance. This

would include supplements of vitamins and minerals, such as vitamin D and calcium. Steak, stew beef, chicken, turkey, liver, kidney and heart are among the adult ocelot's staple foods. Some exotics prefer their food raw while others will eat only cooked food. Also popular with some are egg yolks and cheese.

Occasionally the ocelot should be given grass or similar greens. These are natural emetics. By vomiting, the cat can remove foreign substances, such as hairballs acquired by his frequent self-washings, from his stomach.

The laws regarding an exotic cat in the home vary from city to city. In many places, the ocelot is considered a domestic pet. As such he will not be restricted. Other areas classify him as a wild animal and therefore subject to regulations. These laws may simply require the owner to register his ownership by obtaining a permit; in other cities, the classification may preclude any ownership at all. Finally there are cities that have not classified the ocelot in any way, and the owner should have no difficulty unless an occurrence frightens his neighbors into filing a complaint with police.

The person who buys an exotic must be willing and able to spend great amounts of time with his pet. He must be prepared to learn all that he can about the cat. He must love his particular cat as he would love a human family member and be prepared to make great sacrifices accordingly. He must have enough money for large veterinary bills should the cat require them. He must be prepared to keep the cat for his entire life. Should the cat be outlawed from the town, the owner must be willing and able to move to another city where his pet is welcome.

The person who makes a good owner does not think of this as a sacrifice. His cat simply comes first, all else—his biting, the ruination of furniture, the possible permanent separation of cat and children, or of cat and other pets, the constant cleaning of his litter boxes, quarters, and sprayed areas so that the home does not become overly offensive; the devious methods of destruction and annoyance that only an exotic can think of—all this is secondary.

The owner when traveling or vacationing must stay only in motels where the cat is acceptable or must leave one family member behind to be with and to care for him. Exotics do not endure well in a boarding cage at the veterinarian's and should never be left there.

Perhaps the ocelot or other exotic can never actually be thought of as a pet but rather, as a project—a very dear project.

If you are thinking in the terms of buying an exotic and if you have no doubts about the problems involved; if you feel that the ocelot is the only animal for you and that no domestic pet can take his place; if you are willing to accept the great responsibilities that go with exotic ownership; if you are willing to lavish love on your particular cat; then buy the exotic. He will be a constant source of enjoyment, frustration, and worry—but with the proper attitude you will have some chance of retaining your sanity.

Robert Peraner

Chapter 6

AMERICA'S CAT

If your Chief Lap Sitter, Fire Alarm and Foot Tripper is an American Shorthair, you are very lucky indeed.

Like most other cats, your American Shorthair will be a

medical marvel—deaf as a post when called from across the room, yet able to hear the pop of a baby-food jar at a hundred yards; can't smell how good those yummy vitamins are but can find the only piece of tuna in four pounds of meat; can't see that dangerously teetering lamp he has just whizzed past, but can spot an infant fly on a ten-foot wall. Yes, indeed—he's all cat. If you're saying, "That sounds just like my cat," no matter what his breed, that's my point. He is every person's cat, the basic, the great granddaddy of them all. You've no doubt heard the phrase, "He's a musician's musician," or "ballplayer's ballplayer." Well, so it is with this fellow. He's a "cat's cat."

The American Shorthair as we know him today comes in a beautiful variety of colors and patterns. Some are

prepared by nature, some by environment and some created by man. To help us understand today's cat, let us look at his ancestors.

The first firm evidence of the cat in his relationship to man comes to us from Egypt. Over five thousand years ago, the Egyptians tamed and trained what may have been small jungle cats. The tawny undercoat, mixed with brown and black stripes and spots common to the jungle, is a beautiful and effective camouflage to this day.

Egypt was the grain-growing center of that era. Then as now, mice pilfered grain and cats in turn stalked rodents. Thus was born the love between man and cat.

Evidence of cat history in China, India, and Japan dates back some two thousand years. At some historical point, shorthair cats rescued the silk of Japan just as they had saved the grain of Egypt. The adventures of man became the cat's adventures too. As man migrated, so did the feline guardian of his agriculture.

We know that the Romans and their armies traveled with the cat. We can follow his progress through Europe and eventually into America. He was then and is today a valued crew member of seagoing ships. His job as rodent

controller was even more critical aboard ship than on land. Many a voyage might have been doomed without his help, including the one that brought the pilgrims to our shores. Cats were aboard the Mayflower. With our knowledge of migrating man and cat, the Continental Drift Theory and other evidence, might we not conjecture that the American Indian had a few cats of his own who met the first feline settlers in Plymouth?

These first shorthair cats in America were here on business. They were bred more for ruggedness, hunting ability, intelligence and stamina than for beauty of color, type and pattern. In the mid 1800's shorthairs were still drawing their biggest value dollarwise as hunters. However, by the early 1890's the shorthair was also being prized for his beauty. By 1895, when the first National Cat Show was held at Madison Square Garden, he was well represented in number as well as variety of color.

The breed known in those days was the only shorthair on the continent and his name was description enough. With the importation of other shorthair breeds it became necessary to add the prefix "domestic" to distinguish him

from the imported variety. Since he was domestically perfected in this country, his crown was a proud one to wear. Sadly, however, it gradually came to encompass any domestic cat—regardless of parentage. The accidental matings of domestic and Siamese and Persian were sold by a few unscrupulous breeders as the purebred shorthair. This unhappy circumstance gradually placed a stigma on the name. Finally the concerned breeders and admirers of this fine cat, anxious to restore him to his rightful place in the public eye, voted to give him his well deserved name— American Shorthair.

Technically the American Shorthair is a selectively bred cat, with a definite standard for his well-knit, powerful body, heavy chest and shoulders, medium length and heavily muscled legs. His expressive face has a squared muzzle, firm chin, wide-set ears which are rounded slightly at the tips. His bright round eyes lend this cat his aura

of attentiveness. He has a wide variety of colors and patterns that include solid white, black, blue, red, cream or chinchilla, shaded silver, black smoke and blue smoke. This standard takes care of his visual appeal, but only the cat himself can touch your heart with the warmth and love he has to give. When he gives you the soothing velvet of his purr and caresses your legs with the curl of his body, he belies his ruggedness and reveals the size of his heart. When he sits quietly, eyes narrowed in mystery, you'll wonder if he is of this world and its future, or is just remembering his long and majestic past. When he seeks a high perch for his rest and mimicks his jungle ancestors, his warm eyes still show years of love and service to man.

If your house is graced by the presence of any cat, you are one of the fortunate ones. If your cat is an American Shorthair, your home is full of love.

Virginia Wolfe

Chapter 7

THE ABYSSINIAN CAT

The origin of the Abyssinian cat is obscure, surrounded by mystic stories and legends. Many believe it descends from the Sacred Cat of Egypt and, if one studies statuettes of the Goddess Bastet, there certainly is a strong likeness to the handsome Abyssinian.

The breed, as we know it today, comes from cats taken home by British soldiers from Ethiopia in 1868. An Abyssinian was exhibited in Boston in 1909, perhaps the first in North America, but not until 1935 is there any record of kittens being raised.

Now there is great demand for the breed, both in the show ring and as pets. Owners agree that the Abyssinian is beautiful, affectionate, intelligent and quiet—what more could one ask of a cat?

When born, the tiny kittens are black and orange in color. Within six weeks, the characteristic banding begins to appear in the fur. An individual hair from the back of an adult Abyssinian will show at least three bands of color, the part closest to the skin being a deep russet color, or ruddy, as it is called in the Cat Fancy. The next

band is beige and the very tip of the hair is black. The overall appearance of the fur of a fully ticked cat rather resembles that of a wild rabbit, except that it is more orange. Basically this is the "agouti" pattern found in many wild animals—a perfect camouflage for the cat out-doors where he will easily blend with a background of earth, sand and stones. He will also show to advantage in the sunshine, when his coat will appear as shot silk. A great basker, he will seek a sun-drenched spot anywhere in the house, often moving from window to window as the day progresses.

The Abyssinian's color will continue to improve for the first year, maybe even longer. When fully mature he should have a deep burnt-sienna hue to his undersides.

The color from the base of his fur should shine through almost as though he had swallowed a light bulb.

Few cats are free from barring on the legs and neck. Some fanciers say they prefer cats with the "jewelry" markings, the necklace and bracelets; however, it is a fault to have these markings in the show ring and breeders have worked hard to produce a clear, colorful cat. The coat does not lie sleek as in some other short-haired breeds, but should have a definite bounce to it—soft, silky and resilient. Muscular and agile, this cat can move with amazing speed and is always interested in his surroundings. A good description of the Abyssinian is found in the CFA standard, as follows.

The head is a modified, slightly rounded wedge without flat planes, the brow, cheek and profile lines all showing a gentle contour. There should be a slight rise from the bridge of the nose to the forehead, which should be of good size with width between the ears and flowing into the arched neck without a break. The muzzle is not sharply pointed. Allowance should be made for jowls in adult males.

The ears are alert, large and moderately pointed, broad and cupped at the base and set as though listening. The hair on the ears is very short and close-lying, preferably tipped with black or dark brown. The eyes of an Abyssinian are almond-shaped, large, brilliant and expressive, neither round nor Oriental.

Abyssinian conformation strikes a medium between the extremes of the cobby and the svelte type. Proportion and general balance are more to be desired than mere size. The legs are proportionately slim and fine-boned, with small, oval and compact paws. When standing, the cat gives an impression of being on tiptoe. Toes should number five in front and four behind. The tail is thick at the base, fairly long and tapering.

The Abyssinian coat is soft, silky, fine in texture, but dense and resilient to the touch, long enough to accommodate two or three bands of ticking. The general condition of the cat should be lithe, hard and muscular, giving the appearance of activity, sound health and general vigor. He should be gentle and amenable to handling.

Winners will be withheld in the show ring for a white locket, or white anywhere other than the nostril, chin and upper throat areas, kinked or abnormal tail, a dark unbroken necklace, gray-black hair with no ruddy undercoat, or the incorrect number of toes. The cats will be penalized for off-color pads, a long narrow head or short round head, barring on legs, rings on the tail, or coldness or gray tones in the coat.

Abyssinians come in two colors: ruddy and red. The ruddy coat is ticked with various shades of darker brown or black. The extreme outer tip should be the darkest. The tail is tipped with black and should be without rings. The nose leather of a ruddy Abyssinian should be tile red and the paw pads black or brown. Eye color should be gold or green.

The red Aby is a warm and glowing shade distinctly ticked with chocolate brown. The red's nose leather is rosy pink and the paw pads are also pink, with chocolate brown between the toes, extending slightly beyond the paws. As in the ruddy Aby, the eye color should be gold or green, the richer and deeper the better.

Being an affectionate little fellow, the Abyssinian is almost demanding in his search for human companionship. He is not satisfied merely to sit on a lap, he wants to be up under his owner's chin, purring, "kneading" with his front paws, nuzzling and often making little chirping noises of contentment. If you choose one of this breed for a pet, be prepared to share everything with him—your bed, your food (he will undoubtedly prefer yours to his own, your bath and even your chores if you keep house. He is convinced that bedmaking is a game invented for his benefit. Fond of water, he will want to sit on the edge of your bathtub and dunk his paw, and nothing gives him greater pleasure than a dripping faucet.

As parents, the Abyssinians are unequaled. The stud cat is gentle and loving with his offspring, often baby sitting while mamma takes a few minutes of rest from the family. The mother is attentive and devoted but will defend her family aggressively if occasion arises. The young kits are very active, often climbing out of their basket when less than three weeks old. The kittens appreciate toys. They learn rapidly and love to have a variety of balls, catnip mice and a small cardboard box with holes cut in each side for hide-and-seek.

An Abyssinian cat loves food and normally will not be a fussy eater. Although he drinks water most of the time, he will appreciate an occasional dish of milk.

The coat requires little attention other than a daily light brushing with a very soft baby brush and a brisk rubdown with bare hands to remove loose hair. When he is losing his winter coat, the use of a fine-toothed comb will help, but no harsh grooming is ever necessary.

Normally a hardy and healthy cat, the Aby should still see a veterinarian regularly for a checkup. He will need his annual booster shots for feline enteritis and pneumonitis, and his teeth and gums should be carefully examined twice yearly.

Being exceptionally interested in everything around him, the Aby gets into more mischief than many other breeds. Do watch out for everyday hazards around the house, such as very small toys that can be swallowed, also rubber bands, cellophane paper, needles and thread, small pieces of string (especially the ones that were used on that roast of beef at dinner).

An Abyssinian is a great pet and companion. Happiness is a pansy-faced Abyssinian kitten, reaching up to pat your cheek with a velvet-soft paw.

Edna Field

Chapter 8

THE SABLE-COATED BROWN CAT

Satin-smooth, sable brown, robust and muscular, with ten-dollar gold piece eyes and a wonderfully complex disposition, the Burmese is a cat for the connoisseur. This is a man's cat—obviously not feminine or dainty in ap-

pearance, he often makes a conquest of a man who is completely indifferent to the charms of other breeds.

Although the ideal Burmese according to the show standard is medium-sized, his rounded contours, blunt muzzle and sturdy build make him appear larger than he actually is. The standard also calls for a cat who has "surprising weight for his size," a characteristic of the breed.

Burmese owners contend that their pets have an almost human awareness of mood, reacting strongly to the atmosphere of the home. The male Burmese is usually an extrovert, making friends easily, often a ham when seeking attention from family or friends. The female Burmese is often skittish, asking for attention, then playing the flirt when she receives it. Her irritation is all too obvious when she feels she is slighted. Her brother, at this point, will simply roll over and go to sleep.

As I write this, two Burmese kittens are learning their male and female roles on my lap and around my chair. The male has spent much of the last hour jumping into my lap, climbing to my shoulder, nuzzling my neck and generally saying, "I'm here—pay attention—pet me." His sister has been darting through my papers, pulling my skirt, pestering her brother. When I finally put aside my work to pet her, she decided it was time to sleep after all.

Burmese are noted for their jealousy, are rarely ever shy

or timid. When altered at maturity, they are quiet and gentle, demanding no more exercise than even a small apartment can offer. They love warm, protected window-sills for sleeping. Like their cousins, the Siamese, the Burmese hate the cold and while they enjoy playing with water, I have never known one to prefer the outdoors.

They are easy to care for. The beautiful shine of a good Burmese coat is bred into the cat, as is the texture and length of the coat. The best show cats have very short, very silky coats with a patent-leather shine to them. Once you acquire a Burmese with a coat like this, you can maintain it easily with proper diet, sufficient exercise and an occasional brisk rubdown with a rough towel, followed by smoothing down and stroking to remove dead hairs. The average well-petted Burmese house cat will shed so little as to be no problem.

Burmese don't like being left alone too much; they are a sociable cat, enjoying company and the comings and goings of a large family. They get along well with other cats and with dogs, but will often demand the position of "top cat" in the household. If you and your family must be gone much of the time, do consider a pair of cats. Two cats are little more bother than one.

Selecting the right kitten is important. He can mean years of pride and companionship for you. Not too long ago the Burmese was considered an exotic cat and was seen only in metropolitan areas. Today they are the third

largest breed, based on the Cat Fanciers' Association's registration figures. But they are still scarce enough to make them difficult to locate. Rarely available in pet shops, the best kittens will be found by attending a cat show and talking to the Burmese breeders there.

Almost all Burmese offered today are from registered stock. Whether or not you are looking for a registered pet, do select one from registered parentage. This is the only way you can be sure of a purebred Burmese. In the eyes of a breeder there is no such thing as "half-Burmese"— the cat is either all Burmese or it is not Burmese at all. Selecting from a reputable cattery permits you to see the mother and the rest of the kittens in the litter, and sometimes the sire also. In this way you can more easily visualize what your special kitten will be like when grown. Because the Burmese as a breed are relatively new to this country and because for many years they were quite inbred, they have retained strong family patterns of appearance and behavior.

The first Burmese cat arrived in this country in 1930. She was a young female named Wong Mau, said to have been brought into New Orleans by a sailor. Eventually the cat was given to Dr. Joseph C. Thompson of San Francisco, who fortunately realized that she was unusual. He set about to perpetuate the breed. Details of an experimental program were worked out with the able assistance of serious breeders and geneticists.

Dr. Thompson's two major problems were the lack of a Burmese male and the fact that Wong Mau herself was a Burmese-Siamese hybrid. However, a line of cats was produced to breed true for the Burmese coat.

Wong Mau herself, as seen in old photographs, was a small cat and not especially pretty. Her daughter Topaz Mau was large and beautiful, almost identical to many fine Burmese in shows today.

No one seeing his first Burmese can remain unimpressed. This is not a cat that sidles into a room. The Burmese demands center stage and then, like a precocious child, pretends indifference to all attention. He is the only solid brown cat in nature. The alleys of America produce cats in a rainbow of colors, but never in solid brown or even predominantly brown. Extremely short, fine and satiny in texture, glossy to the point of looking oiled when the cat is seen in a good light, a fine Burmese coat has been compared to a seal coming out of the water.

I have never seen a shy Burmese kitten. Looking very much like small brown bear cubs, they prance about stiff-legged, tails erect and slightly bushed, sniffing, pawing, investigating everything in sight. Faced with an older cat, they will assume it is friendly and invariably extend an affectionate paw. If the older cat does not respond too well, the kitten may dash to the safety of your ankles, but he will soon try again. The Burmese does not hide under a couch or retreat to the bedroom if activity is going on.

Burmese make wonderful parents. The mothers are proud of their babies but do not carry possessiveness to extremes. The family unit is most apparent when several generations of Burmese are housed together. At the present time I have a litter of Burmese, their mother and their grandmother grouped around my feet. The grandmother was spayed at the time the kittens were born, as we felt that her age entitled her to a peaceable life. However, spaying did not remove the strong mother instinct. Upon her return from the veterinarian's, she immediately climbed into the kitten box and gave the babies, then twelve hours old, a thorough washing from head to tip of tail. This was done with a steady series of guttural comments to her daughter, the mother of the kittens, concerning the poor job the daughter had been doing. Attempts to remove her met with no success.

Today the kittens are four weeks old, and it would be hard to tell which cat is the mother. Now that they are eating and the nursing job is almost over, both females mother the babies equally and the grandmother is perhaps the more intense in her devotion to them.

Going along with this familial pattern, the male Burmese is fond of his babies and the mother will seldom display displeasure at his presence at kittening time or afterwards—assuming, of course, that he is a household cat and not a stranger. Heaven help any strange cat who interferes with the kittens.

There is no breed quicker and more violent in attacking intruders on the family circle. A really angry Burmese is a fearsome sight. For this reason, breeders recommend that a new cat be introduced into the household with caution. Never give the Burmese occasion to feel displaced.

Most breeders will try to discourage the novice from breeding Burmese. While nothing is sweeter than a Burmese baby or Burmese pet, nothing is harder to cope with than a calling Burmese female or spraying Burmese male. Burmese females are sexy. Like the Siamese, they are extremely vocal in their demands for an active love life. The noise level produced by just one female in season is sure to bring strong comments from neighbors and loved ones alike. If, despite all recommendations to the contrary, you decide you simply must breed Burmese yourself, do acquire all the information and advice you can before you start. Plenty of advice is available, most of it free. Just be sure to ask *before* buying your cat—not afterwards.

In any case, the next time you think of a kitten, consider the little brown bears of the cat world, talk to someone who owns a Burmese, and you will be convinced that only with a Burmese can your family be entirely complete.

Mrs. Ralph M. (Patricia) Robie

Chapter 9

THE BIRMAN IS THE SACRED CAT OF BURMA

It is said that the Sacred Cats were originally raised in the temples of Burma. In the mid-1920's, a pair of them was smuggled out of a temple and brought to France. Another pair may have followed shortly thereafter. Since then, Birmans have been raised in western Europe, all descending from the original pair, or two pairs.

During World War II, the Sacred Cat almost became extinct. Fortunately, a few pairs remained in France and

Italy. After the war, the breed slowly increased again. This is to the good. The Birman is too rare, too interesting, too excellent to be allowed to fade.

The gloves on the Sacred Cat of Burma are considered the most important physical feature. They should be full at the wrist or ankle joint and symmetrical and pure. Eye color should be a dark blue, almost purple. The blue point may have lighter eyes. The diamond-shaped face mask, the ears and the tail (which should be thick and bushy) must be the same color. The dark seal point should be almost black; the blue point, a beige-blue-gray.

The ruff, or collar, should be full and thick. It should stand up and be light, almost white, in color. Body color should be as light as possible. Over the flanks and shoulders, the coloration should be a little darker. Ears are medium-sized.

In ancient Burma it is said that loving care and attention was given to the white-gloved temple cats because of

the Burmese belief in reincarnation. After death, they felt, their priests returned in the form of these sacred cats.

The Temple of Leo Tsum was set by a lovely lake in a valley surrounded by mountains. It housed a golden goddess with shining sapphire eyes. Her name was Tsun-Kyan-Kse and her duty was to watch the transmutation of souls. Mun-Ha, one of the most admired of the priests, often knelt before her in meditation, his beautiful and faithful white cat, Sinh, always by his side.

One night while he knelt as the moon rose, raiders attacked the temple and killed the good priest. At the moment of Mun-Ha's death, Sinh placed his paws upon his master and faced the goddess. Immediately the white hairs of his body became as golden as she was. His eyes became sapphire blue. On his four legs, the light color shaded downward to a deep, velvety brown except where the four paws rested on his adored master's body. There the white color still remained as a sign of purity.

In the morning, the raided temple shone with golden

light. The other temple cats, like Sinh, reflected a golden hue. Sinh never left his position. After his master's death, he continued to gaze steadily into the eyes of the goddess. Seven days later, the faithful animal also died and carried with him into paradise the soul of Mun-Ha.

It is written: "Woe to anyone who even unwittingly puts an end to one of these worshipped cats. The worst punishment will be in store for him, and his guilty, tortured soul will find no rest for the whole of eternity."

Only a few, and they must be proved worthy, are permitted to possess one of these beautiful creatures.

In my fifty years in the Cat Fancy, I have never had better companions than the Birmans. To know the Sacred Cat has been one of my life's great joys.

Verner Clum

Chapter 10

REX—THE CURLY, CUDDLY CLOWN

The curly-coated Rex—even its whiskers curl— appeared as a spontaneous mutation in several widely separate parts of the world. Of eleven known occurrences, five have survived and are being actively bred, each representing a distinct and separate mutation.

In appearance the Rex is elegant, trim and racy. Even the males look dainty—except in play. The Rex is a study in curves. The body is arched, the hips rounded. The tail is carried in a circle.

The coat is neither harsh nor woolly. To the touch it is soft, smooth and plush. Though rarely over half an inch in length, the individual hairs are finer than silk thread. Body warmth to the touch is more apparent in the Rex than in other cats. The cat is easy to pet. Fortunately he is affectionate and loves being stroked.

The fragile appearance masks a firm, muscular body. This cat has been described as "steel covered with velvet" or a "lead pipe covered with down." Marj Estes aptly describes them as "the Maxi cat with the Mini coat."

Martha Myrick wrote, "The idea of a cat whose fur looked as if treated by an old-fashioned marcel iron at first repelled me, but then I stroked one, and once having felt the strange cut-velvet texture of the Rex cat, I was hooked."

Both longhaired and shorthaired cats are normally coated. The normal coat consists of guard hair or outer coat, awn hairs (mid coat) and down hairs (undercoat). The Rex coat, on the other hand, consists of down hair or undercoat only in most cases. In some Rex both down hair and awn hair may be found, but as even the awn hair on the Rex is shorter and finer than normal, the coat will appear to consist of down hair only. The Rex cat has no guard hair.

The tightness of the wave can vary. We have had as many as five different degrees of wave in a litter of six kittens. The coat will also vary on the individual from time to time due to kittening, extremely warm weather or diet. Whatever the wave, the coat always retains its beguiling silken feel.

The first Rex to be discovered was the Cornish kitten Kallibunker, a cream-colored male in a litter of ordinary shorthairs. He was born in 1950 on a farm in Bodmin Moor, Cornwall, England. His mother was a normal-coated shorthair tortoiseshell cat. The father was unknown.

The owner, Mrs. Nina Ennismore, realizing that he was unusual, sought the advice of her veterinarian, who suggested she consult a geneticist. She was put in touch with Dr. A. C. Jude and Dr. A. G. Searle and with their help and that of Sterling Webb, a program was begun to perpetuate the Rex as a true breed.

mari

Kallibunker was mated back to his mother. Several curly-coated kittens resulted. He was also bred to normal-coated queens other than his mother and normal-coated kittens were the outcome. The normal-coated, half-Rex kittens, when bred together or to the kittens from Kallibunker and his mother, produced litters of normal and curlies in 1.1 to 1.3 ratios. And when curly was bred to curly, all curly kittens were the result.

The second important Rex discovery was Lammchen, discovered in 1951 in Germany by Dr. Scheur-Karpin. Lammchen, a tortoiseshell, was similar to the Cornish Rex in general appearance. A breeding program was instigated and thus the German Rex mutation was also retained.

In 1951 there was said to be a Rex in Italy. In the mid-1950's a Rex was reported in France. Unfortunately, these two strains, along with the Rex found in Ohio in 1952, have not been heard about since and were apparently lost. The third and fourth retained discoveries were in the United States.

The fifth remaining mutation was the Devon Rex. Kirlee was found in Devonshire in 1960 by Beryl Cox. It was felt for a while that he and Kallibunker were of the same mutation, until crossbreeding produced normal-coated kittens. They were two different mutations.

In 1951, *Life* magazine carried a picture of an exotic and saucy kitten with curly whiskers and coat. Mrs. Fran Blancheri of San Diego, California, traced the picture to the owner in England. She was finally able in 1957 to buy two of these unusual cats from Mrs. Ennismore and have them sent to the United States.

Penndennis Castle, the red tabby male, was sterile, possibly because of illness when a kitten. The lovely blue female, La Morna Cove, had fortunately been bred before leaving England to her brother, Pildhu. Shortly after her arrival in California, she produced the kittens that became the backbone of many beautiful Rex lines in the United States.

In San Bernardino, California, at about the same time, two more curly cats were found in an animal shelter, a mother and her kitten, parentage unknown. The mother, Mystery Lady, was a calico, with one blue eye and one gold eye. Her coat was similar to the Cornish Rex except for length. Where the Cornish Rex coat was from one-fourth to a half inch long, Mystery Lady's coat was one-half to three inches long. She was, in the opinion of the veterinarians who examined her, two or three years old.

Her kitten was a red male. Dwana Sumi was the same Rex type as his mother, but with a rounder head. His coat was a good inch to an inch and a half long. Dwana Sumi was bred once to his mother. The one kitten from this breeding, Franchini, a red female, had a coat nearly as long as her sire's. For this reason, neither Sumi nor Franchini was used in the Rex breeding. We named them

Marcel cats, and tried unsuccessfully for several years to have someone work with them. They were eventually placed as pets.

Meanwhile, several breeders were trying to establish Rex in the United States. We felt that even though two mutations were incompatible in the first generation, producing normal-coated kittens (as did all Rex when outcrossed, no matter how bred), we would be way ahead, more likely to retain the curl, by using the California mutant, Mystery Lady, as our outcrossing.

Mystery Lady was therefore bred to the Cornish-Kallibunker line through a descendent of La Morna Cove. The resultant kittens when bred to each other produced three kittens, all curly. Our percentage of curly stayed at three to one and of course, when curly was bred to curly, all curly were produced. Through the years, we have felt that our gamble paid off. And when Grand Champion Rodell's Ravenesque became the highest scoring and top winning Rex cat ever, the best Shorthair Female in the United States in 1968-1969, we were delighted.

Within the last year two new mutations have been found, one in northern California and one in the east.

Of more importance than his origin, to those interested in the Rex, is his sweet and loving personality. We have owned cats since childhood. A cavalcade of most breeds and some halfbreeds has run through my life, but none has had the sweetness, the sincere affection and obvious wish to please that the Rex has. The happy temperament and sense of humor are especially enjoyable.

Another unusual trait of the Rex is that many will wag their tails when happy, as dogs do.

They mature early and breed from eight or nine months. They are seldom as highly sexed as some other breeds and, because of the sweet, muted, birdlike voice, do not disturb when in season with raucous calling. We have read that some Rex have a sterility problem, but have never had this problem with our own cats.

They are exceptionally healthy, have excellent appetites and will thrive on any good balanced diet. They do need supplements of oil more than other breeds to keep their coats in curl and condition. Although grooming is practically unnecessary, a fine-toothed baby or flea comb should be run through the coat at least once a week. We also advise bathing frequently as they have no outer slick coat to repel soil.

Unlike most breeds, whose history is lost in fable and legend, this newest true breed of cat has documented background. Yet an element of mystery remains.

Evelyn Kieler has suggested that Rex is a reincarnation. Egyptian cats of the Saite-Ptolemaic period, 600 to 300 B.C., were sometimes slick. We can also see the resemblance to copies of the statue in the Louvre. Again the question surfaces—how long and how often has this type of mutation been cropping up?

Dell Thetford Smith

Chapter 11

THE BALINESE IS MY CAT

Well, here we are at the Cat Show. I sit beside my four drowsing Balinese beauties. Everybody stops. The long, soft, silky fur, that noble look, have intrigued them. I smile encouragingly. I want them to know our cats. I answer questions.

Visitor: "What is a Balinese?"

Exhibitor: "It is a longhaired Siamese."

Visitor: "Oh. I didn't know they had longhaired Siamese."

Exhibitor: "Well, they are rather rare. The breed is about fifteen years old."

Visitor: "Do they really come from Bali?"

Exhibitor: "No, not really. But they do have the Siamese background, which is oriental. And they do

have the delicate, exotic look of Balinese dancers. So the pioneers of the breed felt that the name Balinese would be right for them."

Visitor: "What is their temperament like? Is it like the other Siamese?"

Exhibitor: "You will not find a sweeter-tempered or more intelligent cat."

Visitor: "Are the coats hard to care for?"

Exhibitor: "No. The coat lies naturally and does not have to be fluffed up like the Persian coat. We keep an eye on it for tangles but rarely find any. A little daily stroking and ruffling with the hand, and a light brushing and combing, is enough."

Visitor: "What is the difference between a Balinese and a Himalayan?"

Exhibitor: "The Himalayan came originally from a cross between a Persian and a Siamese. But a Balinese is a true Siamese cat. It must have nothing but Balinese or Siamese in its pedigree. No other longhair cross is permitted."

Visitor: "Where did the long hair come from?"

Exhibitor: "It just popped up. A fluffy little changeling shows up occasionally among its shorthaired

brothers and sisters in a normal Siamese litter. If these little ones are bred to longhairs from other Siamese litters, they will produce longhaired kittens."

The ideal Balinese is a svelte, dainty cat with long, tapering lines, lithe but muscular. The general impression should be aristocratic, with a long, fine head held alert, ears pricked forward, general conformation that of a Siamese.

Long and abundant whiskers are characteristic. The temperament should be happy, lively, and affectionate, easy to handle and care for.

Every year since 1963 there have been Balinese winners of All-Sectional and All-American awards. These lovely cats are now shown and judged among their peers in the longhair championship classes—as they indeed deserve to be.

Sylvia Moberly Holland

Chapter 12

THE RUSSIAN BLUE, KING OF THE SHORTHAIRS

I like to think of Russian Blues as graceful, engaging, attractive and loyal. There are many speculative stories about their origin. One is that they descended from the archangel cat of Northern Russia. However, the best bloodlines today are found in Sweden and England. The foremost cats in Sweden are in the Kabbarps Cattery. England has the Dunloe line. The cat has been bred in the United States since 1907.

The Russian Blue of today is a shorthair, bluish gray in color with silver tipping on the fur. No markings, stripes or white hairs are permitted. When young, the color of the eyes is yellow, but in full maturity the eyes should be a vivid emerald green. The fur is so dense that it gives a massive appearance. When lifted, the cat will be found fine-boned and strong-muscled. He is as hardy as he looks. He is not a finicky eater. He is easy to take care of and enjoys being groomed.

Many ask, "Is it true that they are voiceless?" They are not loud like the Siamese but are quite capable of making their wants known. They will actually converse with you. And when in season they behave much the same way as any other cat.

The Russian Blue makes a game of disappearing, yet he is always within reaching distance—so he can hear you but not be seen. He is famous for hide-'n-seek.

A specialty of one of my females in the cattery is to deliberately push up a ceiling tile to get into the rafters. She manages to put the tile back in place so that one has no idea where to start looking. Yet she will finally answer when called—that is, when she is tired of the game—and will holler loud and long to come down. When you find her you never fail to be impressed with her sweet expression and the shape of her mouth. Is she really smiling at you?

The Russian Blue is dignified, proud and graceful. Once you have owned one you will never be without a Russian Blue in your home.

Dorothy Lech

Chapter 13

WHAT—NO TAIL!

If your cat is a Manx, you have one of nature's most unusual felines. The Manx is believed to have developed on the Isle of Man, west of the British coast, but there is no documented proof of his presence there until 1820. So the historical background of the Manx is just as mysterious as his taillessness.

Actually, not all Manx cats are tailless. There are three types, and two of these have tails. The show Manx are tailless and are called rumpies; those having a short tail are called stumpies; and those bearing a full-length tail, longies. All three types have the characteristic bone structure and double coat. One legend has it that Manx tails were used to decorate warriors' hats—and each mother cat, in order to save her young, bit off their tails. The more scientific theory is that the tailless factor is an incomplete dominant. This means the mutation tends to perpetuate itself when bred with cats that have tails.

Continuous breeding of rumpy to rumpy will produce weak kittens and deformities. Regardless of what type Manx is used for breeding, the potential for tailless kittens is present. The typical Manx litter consists of one rumpy, one stumpy, and one longie.

A pure Manx need not be tailless. He has other characteristics. His high, muscular hindquarters give his back a decided downward slope. His walk is close to a waddle and his running is a hop similar to a rabbit. The hindquarters are extremely full and powerful, giving him a fantastic ability to leap great heights in the air. The build of a Manx can be compared with that of a quarter horse or bulldog. The body is short and compact, with a heavy neck and muscular hindquarters. The head must be round, complimenting the overall strength of the body.

The Manx has a lush coat and an ability to shed it at will. A Manx that is frightened and upset will loosen its coat and squirm away, leaving a handful of hair.

Many cats are one-person cats, really devoted to their chosen one, and they follow their masters everywhere and carry on quite a conversation. The Manx will ask for attention or tell what he thinks with a variety of chirps. He can be jealous of other Manx if he feels slighted—but let in another cat of a different breed and be prepared for all-out battle.

The breed is close to extinction as these cats are difficult to breed, not prolific and do not flourish. There are several devoted Manx breeders in the United States and a government-owned and operated cattery on the Isle of Man. Perhaps in years to come, the breed will gain the popularity and attention it deserves.

My desire to have a registered cat began in 1965, at a cat show. I fell irrevocably in love with the Manx. Studying everything I could find about them, I realized that I faced a real challenge. The problems associated with the cat seemed too overwhelming for any but a few dedicated breeders.

My family came to my aid. The initial step and encouragement can be credited to my father, for his advice in buying a good-quality cat and keeping the breed pure. A six-month-old female was the starting point for all our future Manx. When Shortie arrived at the airport, I'm sure I was the more nervous of the two of us.

After four months, we decided to buy Shortie a mate. This wasn't simple. We wanted a male who was already siring. Eventually we settled on a seven-month-old male who suited our needs even though he was still quite young. He and Shortie are still producing our best kittens.

When someone requests one of my Manx, I have a two-sided problem to consider. Does the person want a conversation piece, or would he understand the emotional make-up of the Manx?

The Manx is not just anyone's cat. When a person takes a Manx, both must have suitable personalities. It's not that the cat must suit the person; the person must suit the cat.

A common experience of the Manx fancier is selling a kitten only to have it returned because when approached, even on the owner's knees, the kitten would only run and hide. The Manx must be allowed to choose his person; then he is usually happy. He must not be ignored or rejected, or he will be miserable and so will the owners.

I will not agent or ship my cats. They are one-person cats and do not respond well in difficult situations.

If you want a cat for a companion, a Manx will always be with you, watching everything you do and talking continually. Some even go so far as to break through a screen door to reach you on the other side.

The Manx is appreciative. They always say "please" and "thank you."

The Manx is ideal for a single person, or a family with older children who give him his just dues. His personality expands when he is the center of the family attention. The Manx, to be at his best, must be an integral part of the family.

He also needs an outdoor, fresh-air atmosphere. Our cats are housed in large cages during the day and are allowed to exercise in the runs during the cooler evening.

My reason for showing Manx is to stimulate appreciation of the breed. I want people to notice the Manx as a quality cat. To accomplish this, I attend as many CFA shows as time and distance permit, to present the Manx at his fine and characteristic best.

Margaret M. Thompson

Chapter 14

CHOOSE THE KORAT . . . THE GOOD LUCK CAT!

The Korat, a native of Thailand, is a shorthair with silver-blue coat and huge green-gold or amber-green eyes in a heart-shaped face. In Thailand, the silver sheen is called sea foam.

The name Si-Sawat (see-sahwaat) is used for these cats in their homeland. "Si" means color. A wild fruit, called the "Look Sawat," has a seed the same shade as the cat. The Korat coat color does not alter. The color at birth is the same as at death. Any white patches on the underside (a fault) are obvious at birth. Scattered white hairs may appear later from spots that have been vaccinated, or from injury.

In the jungle villages of Thailand, Korat cats are used as watchdogs. A disturbance causes the cat to stand stiff-legged, facing the source, uttering wailing cries interspersed with warning clicking sounds. The Korat is believed to bring good fortune to his owner—if a farmer, good crops, for the cat is cloud-colored with eyes the color of young rice; if a merchant, the cat brings prosperity (silver). A gift of a Korat cat to a bride ensures a fortunate marriage.

In the National Museum in Bangkok, an ancient manuscript hangs. Known as the "Smud Koi" or "Papyrus Book," it contains a series of paintings of cats of Siam. Each cat is described by a verse. The verse for our Korat says:

"The cat 'Maled' has a body like 'Doklao'
The hairs are smooth with roots like clouds and tips
like silver.
The eyes shine like dewdrops on a lotus leaf."

Say Dok like rock and lao like now. Dok means flower.
Lao is a kind of wild herb, like lemongrass, with silver-
tipped flowers. "Doklao" is a pretty way of referring to
hair that is silvering—"silver threads among the gold."

People ask, "Where has the Korat cat been all these
years?" The Korat cat has been in his native Thailand—
and in Occidental countries, too! A Korat cat was exhibited in England, at Holland House, London, as early
as 1896, by a Mr. Spearman. In 1906, a Mr. Robins of
New York City (it states in *The Journal of Cat Genetics*)
attested to the existence of these silver-blue cats in the
Korat Plateau or northeastern part of Thailand. Refer-

ences may be found to their presence in the United States in the 1930's and 1940's.

The Korat cat has been cherished in Thailand for centuries because of his beauty, sweet disposition, prowess as a fighter and the good luck he brings. A crook or kink in the tail means added good luck. The purists want straight-tailed cats. The average pet owner goes for a crook tail.

The cats are rare even in Thailand. At one time, they were never sold, only given as a mark of esteem or respect. Now that there is a growing interest in this breed around the world, the cats are sometimes for sale at inflated prices.

In March, 1965, all known breeders of Korats were asked to send in a full description of their cats. From these, a proposed judging standard was compiled.

This standard goes into great detail. The head when viewed from the front is heart-shaped with breadth between the eyes, greatly curving to a well-developed but not sharply pointed muzzle. The forehead is large and flat. In the male there is an indentation in the center of the forehead. The chin and jaw are strong. In profile there is a slight stop between forehead and nose. The nose is short and has a slight downward curve. The ears are large with a rounded tip and large flare at the base, set high on the head, giving an alert expression. Inside, the ears are sparsely furnished.

The body is blue all over, tipped with silver, the more silver the better, without shading or tabby markings. Where the coat is short the sheen of the silver is intensified. The paw pads are dark blue ranging to lavender with a pinkish tinge. The nose and lip leather is dark blue or lavender. The eyes are large and luminous. They are prominent, wide open and oversized for the face. They have an Asian slant when partially closed. The eye color is brilliant green or amber-green.

There were in 1965 six known imports. More began arriving. The Korat Cat Fanciers Association insists on proof of authentic Thai origin by means of a pedigree, air waybill, or ship's manifest, customs papers, health certificate issued by a veterinarian in Thailand, or rabies and enteritis vaccination certificates issued in Thailand. The Association does not "recognize" cats that cannot prove Thai origin, and members do not permit any breedings of their Korats with any other breed with the intent to call the offspring Korats. To keep the Korat as it is, a native, natural breed, they keep a record of all Korats born here, purchased and otherwise placed, and imported.

A peculiarly strong bond of affection exists between Korats and their owners in this country as well as in Thailand. These cats are extremely responsive. They are demanding, too. They don't thrive when set aside. We don't encourage owners of many multiple breeds to add Korats to their families as this conglomeration is sometimes a failure—the Korat isn't happy.

They like to be participators. There is no household activity that isn't enlivened with inspection, supervision, mere stopping by to visit, or sometimes a thump or two from a Korat paw. Most of them answer only when spoken to and are not chatterboxes. But if you like your cats to be ornamental but not intrusive, Korats should not be your choice. One of mine walks back and forth across my typewriter as I type (actually, they all do it), then he gets busy pawing the envelopes and stationery out of the drawer. He can't abide a closed door—he has to open it and enter. On a busy day, he may spend a lot of time shut in a cupboard as a result!

I went to Bangkok for five wonderful weeks, visiting Cat People and seeing the sights. I was impressed by the serenity of the male cats there. I didn't see one nervous, pacing male. I don't know how to account for this. Perhaps some of us here make our cats too dependent on us, even though their responsiveness is hard to ignore. Some of the cats in Thailand were in large cages, some were free and some were loose in the home in a "pride" community. One adult male snoozed on the counter of a bookbinder's store, where people came and left through two wide open doorways. Anyone could pet him. He purred.

Cats in Bangkok are generally fed meat and rice or fish and rice. The rice is polished and white, but the fish is loaded with minerals and nutritive properties. Dr. Jit Waramontri, a Bangkok veterinarian, told me that cases of rickets in cats there are rare.

Arranging for the transportation of cats from Thailand, I found, is not simple. Carriers had to be made. Food for the journey was hard to find. I located several jars of strained baby meats and provided food and water dishes for each cat. Detailed instructions were written on each carrier. In spite of all this preparation, whoever fed them at Honolulu neglected to remove their food and water dishes from the carriers afterward. As a result, I landed in Los Angeles with wet, shivering cats. This added instruction should be included among directions for the handling of cats in transit, where there are stops when feeding can take place, so that the cats' dishes will be removed, emptied and placed in the bag provided to carry their food, for re-use at the next stop.

The carriers for the nine cats I brought back from
Thailand with me were made of wood, with wire insets in
front and a wire floor. Under the wire floor was a metal
pull-out tray. Traveling pens were available from the air-
line, but as these were designed for dogs, they were un-
necessarily tall for cats (a cat can sit up comfortably in
possibly half the height a German Shepherd, for instance,
would need). Because one pays for volume weight, the
wooden carriers were more practical. I don't think cats like
to travel in open cages.

There are many instances of the good luck charm working for the Korat owners. As our families increase and we
send out more and more of these cats to new homes, we
are regaled with stories of unexpected good fortune. Part
of the luck of it all is living with one, or with several, as I
do.

Daphne Negus

Chapter 15

THE VELVET HAVANA BROWN

At a show, if you stop to chat while looking at all the
breeds, you may be detained by an outstretched oval paw,
velvet and brown with pink pads. Havana Browns use
their paws to know an object, whereas most cats sniff first.
Turning, you will see brown whiskers and a pink-tinged,
upturned nose.

Having gained your attention, his next step is to pose and preen by rubbing against the cage and exercising claws on the floor covering, followed by a prodigious stretch which shows off his body. He has perfect proportions, neither cobby like other brown cats, nor svelte like the Siamese. Havana fanciers have been diligent in preserving the firm body and exquisite green eye color that contributes so much to this breed's extraordinary attractiveness. Notice the slight forward tilt of the ears and the pansy-like or pixie expression that is singular to Havanas.

Exhilarated by an audience, his next act will probably be acrobatic hanging on the cage like a starfish on a rock. In conclusion, he will plop down, assume the posture of a sphinx, chest on curled front paws, to await the next spectator.

If the owner is free to discuss the breed, the usual first question is, "Why are they called Havana Brown?" The breed is man-made and is not indigenous to Cuba. It originated in England, the result of very selective breeding based on sound genetic principles. The sleekly beautiful

coat suggested the name Havana because of its color—cigar brown. Recognition in championship class was granted by the Governing Council in England and, when imported, the cats were recognized by our national registering associations.

If you are not a fancier, your interest will be in the cat's personality. Cats differ as profoundly as men do. You will find most Havanas are dignified, yet capricious. Like all cats, they possess an independent spirit. The air of subjection is repugnant to their inborn sovereignty.

They are always ready to entertain. They will welcome you by rubbing gently against your legs, knowing we all love the feel of soft fur. If you pick one up to pet, he or she will be polite and accept this tribute for a brief moment. Their play is a choreography of attack and defense, as involved as a ballet. Watching, you realize they have

strict rules. Most of the action is prancing, advancing, teasing one another with a flick of the paw, dancing sideways, rolling and tumbling. Worn out, they will fall exhausted in a hug and lick each other's faces until they fall asleep, purring fervently.

Cats can change your life and Havanas do. In a new home the first thing to know is the location of the sand pan. They have been trained to neatness at an early age by mother. Various voice inflections convey most other wants and you will soon recognize these, such as their authoritative call for food or attention. Once settled in, they find house plants and furniture ideal for hide and seek.

Kittens are fascinated by moving objects and will use their paws to play billiards with anything that rolls. Another sport is "mountain climbing," involving the draperies. Having ascended, they engage in plaintive mewing

for assistance in coming down. Cats do not understand retreat, a fact well known to local fire departments. Another sport is the broad jump—chair to table to desk is a minimum. This is done without toppling the finest bric-a-brac. When they accidently knock something over, they will run and hide to avoid punishment and to cover their embarrassment at having been so awkward. Frequently they volunteer more assistance than is convenient.

They are professional at stealing. You will be amazed at what you will find in the most unusual places—a skein of yarn, a spool of thread from the sewing box, a puff from the vanity, stockings from a hamper, pencils. Unless you have a pencil secured by a chain to the telephone, depend on your memory for taking messages.

Often their antics will bring laughter. This is very disconcerting to the cat, who may leave the room to express his or her indignation.

Long association has made me a humble admirer, not the ultimate authority, and I sincerely hope this portrait has endeared Havanas to you.

Dallas E. Sidlo

Part II

KEEPING CATS HAPPY

Chapter 16

A QUESTION OF FOOD

Q: What should I feed my cat?

A: Try never to forget that the cat, being a small animal, has a small stomach. Concentrated foods and variety are of the utmost importance. Besides the commercially prepared cat food you'll find on your market shelves, there are many specialized cat diets, balanced and prepared for cats, which may be obtained through your veterinarian or your pet shop. Since cats must always have variety, even these specialized diets must be alternated or supplemented with raw meat.

The metabolic processes and nutritional requirements of the carnivorous cat differ greatly from those of the omnivorous human. Infectious diseases flourish when nutrition is inadequate and when raw meat is left out of the diet.

To insure your cat's health, therefore, do not confine yourself to cans of food from the market shelves. Use some steamed fresh fish, cooked poultry, raw muscle meat with fat, liver, kidney and heart. Avoid raw pork. Use cottage cheese, yellow cheese, raw egg yolk, or whole eggs cooked at low temperature (never use raw egg whites), kelp, which is an excellent source of all minerals, powdered and flaked brewer's yeast. Try to make three-fourths of the diet consist of fresh raw food. Use corn oil, wheat germ oil, and other polyunsaturated oils such as safflower oil.

Q: How much should I feed my cat?

A: Four to six ounces of moist food* (i.e., canned food, which is about 30% protein on a dry weight basis) is

enough for the average cat, excluding kittens and pregnant or nursing cats. Pet cats often eat more than they actually need for a variety of reasons, mostly psychological. If your cat is putting on weight, protect his or her health by cutting back on the amount you feed. However, if your cat's weight is abnormally in excess, discuss a diet regime with your veterinarian because drastic reductions in food intake have to be balanced with vitamin and mineral supplements.

Q: How often should I feed my cat?

A: Two meals a day are adequate. In fact, one meal is enough, but pet cats prefer the variety of having their food split between morning and evening. However, do *not* leave food around between meals—even dry food—or you will encourage overeating. If your cat leaves food in his dish, throw it out or store it for next time. Furthermore, all cats learn where the goodies are kept, and will rush up with pleas and demands whenever the refrigerator is opened. For everyone's sake—particularly your cat's—ignore these "Aw, just a little snack!" performances or they will become a bad habit. Let the cat eat as much as he or she wants at mealtime only.

Q: Do cats need water?

A: Definitely! However, they don't drink much on a moist diet such as canned foods, which contain up to seventy percent water. Water should always be available to your cat. Excessive drinking—either suddenly or over a period —is usually a sign of kidney problems and you should tell your veterinarian about it. This increase in drinking is not to be confused with a cat's naturally increased demand for water when he or she is put on dry foods such as kibbles and chows, or when the weather is hot.

Q: I feed my cat on a well-known brand of commercial cat food. All the ads say this is "a complete cat diet." Is this true?

A: No. Cats should not be fed *exclusively* on a commercial canned or packaged diet. Most do not adequately meet all nutritional requirements. A problem arises when a cat develops a perference amounting to addiction for one specific commercial food and refuses all other foods to the point of starvation. Do not allow your cat to fall into this nutritional trap; remember, variety is all-important in a cat's diet.

Q: Is it necessary to give my cat a vitamin or mineral supplement?

A: Cats fed only on commercial cat foods—especially cats fed only one type of such food—will develop deficiencies. These deficiencies are usually not sufficiently extreme to make the cat visibly ill, but they lower his or her resistance to disease. Cats on a vitamin—or mineral—deficient diet are more than usually susceptible to respiratory diseases, skin problems, gum infections and heart lesions. These and related disorders generally reduce the cat's life span.

Vitamin and mineral requirements can be filled by feeding one of the following foods *raw* at least twice a week: liver, kidney, heart, meat, or egg yolks. Fish oils or whole milk should also be fed at least twice a week. Some

commercial foods are well supplemented, but are usually low in vitamin B. Here again, I must stress the importance of variety. Cats who insist on eating a limited diet should be put on a vitamin supplement, but the choice of supplement should be made by your veterinarian.

Q: I feed my cat nothing but meat. Surely this is a more than adequate diet for him?

A: Sorry to disappoint you, but it definitely is not! A meat-only diet—although seemingly of such a high quality as to be beyond criticism—is still deficient in certain ways. For instance, because it is low in calcium, a meat-only diet can cause rickets in kittens. Whole milk and cottage cheese are good sources of calcium, and also of vitamin D. If your cat will only eat meat, then you must provide him with a vitamin and mineral supplement.

Q. Should cats be fed the same food for every meal?

A: No. Many cat owners will discover a particular food that their cat prefers above all others. Cats must have a balanced diet. Cats are great actors and will do everything they can to convince you that they will only eat their favorite food to the exclusion of all else, including not eating for days. If you allow your cat to convince you that he will only eat his favorite food, you will have a very spoiled and probably unhealthy animal.

Q: What should kittens eat?

A: At first, kittens should be fed food similar to mother's milk. Esbilac is good. Gradually they can be fed the same foods as adult cats but in smaller amounts; meat should be cut into smaller pieces. Kittens should be fed at least five times a day until they are four months old. Gradually reduce the number of times per day you feed the kittens until after six months when they can be fed as adult cats.

Q: My cat won't drink milk. How am I going to make up for this lack of calcium and vitamin D in his diet?

A: Many cats do not drink milk. It is not essential, in the sense that there are other sources of calcium and vitamin D. Do not try to force milk on your cat if he doesn't like it. Alternative sources of calcium include bones and many of the commercial foods. Fish oils and butter contain vitamin D. Cats sometimes develop diarrhea from drinking milk. If this happens, you should either stop giving the cat milk altogether, or dilute the milk with an equal volume of water. If the diarrhea clears up on the watered milk formula, you can try gradually reducing the amount of water until the cat is back on whole milk again.

Q: What if I feed my cat nothing but fish? Cats love it, so it must be good.

A: This type of reasoning is similar to assuming that candy must be a good diet for children because they like it so much. Fish is meat and, as you know now, a meat-only diet is not sufficient. Besides, some fish (both commercially canned and raw) destroy essential vitamins in the cat's metabolism and thus bring on skin problems, heart lesions, and a disease known as steatitis. Tuna is the worst offender. Feed your cat fish—even tuna—once or twice a week, but *not* as an exclusive diet. Cats become addicted to tuna, I might add, and it is often necessary to starve

them for up to three days in order to break them of a tuna-only diet.

Q: What is the best diet for cats?

A: A *varied* diet. Fresh raw meat, raw eggs, raw fish, raw liver, raw kidney, raw beef heart, as well as cottage cheese and various cereals (e. g., oatmeal, rice, etc.), should be used in turn to supplement commercial cat foods. However, if your cat will eat only a commercial cat food, you should provide him or her with pharmaceutical vitamin and/or mineral supplements. This is something you should check with your veterinarian, who can advise you regarding the exact requirements that are not being met by the commercial food in question, and hence can prescribe the correct supplements and amounts. Vitamin supplements from your pet store or supermarket may contain too much or too little for your cat's particular requirements. Overdosage with vitamin or mineral supplements can do your cat even more harm than the dietary deficiencies you

wish to correct. A high-fat (i.e., nine percent in canned foods, twenty-five percent in dry foods), high-protein (i.e., ten percent in canned foods, thirty percent in dry foods) diet is best for your cat. Many commercial foods are low in fat because fat has a tendency to turn the food rancid. Consequently, it is generally necessary to supplement your cat's diet with bacon fat, lard, or other saturated fat. Lack of fats, or the use of the wrong fats, often causes skin problems in the cat.

Q: What about dog foods? Can I feed my cat on a good commercial dog food?

A: Yes, you can feed dog food to your cat, but not as an exclusive diet. Although many commercial dog foods are well-balanced diets for dogs, they are not balanced for cats. For one thing, they are too low in protein, fat and B vitamins for cats. The dog's nutritional requirements are quite different from the cat's.

Q: Can I feed my cat baby foods?

A: Baby foods are excellent nutritionally for the cat, but they do tend to cause diarrhea. For this reason, they are best avoided in the normal, healthy cat. Veterinarians like to suggest baby foods for sick cats with poor appetites, since these foods can be given easily via a doll's bottle or eye dropper. The veterinarian is in a position to help control any diarrhea that may result in such instances.

Q: Is there such a thing as malnutrition in cats?

A: Very definitely. This condition can occur at any time in a cat's life. For example, if a mother cat is inadequately nourished, she will produce and raise undernourished kittens. Often this deficiency cannot be reversed in one generation and it may take several generations before normal cats are obtained again. (This is a consideration of paramount importance to breeders, of course.)

One source of vitamin deficiency in kittens, for instance, arises if the mother cat is fed cooked meat instead of raw meat. The veterinarian often sees kittens with distended stomachs suffering from clinical starvation, a condition due to the kittens' efforts to obtain sufficient calories for their needs by eating huge quantities of low-calorie commercial foods. Some of these commercial foods have such a high percentage of water, ash and bone, and such a low calorific value, that no normal kitten can find room in his stomach for the volume which will provide him with enough calories.

The same condition can occur in adult cats, although their calorific and vitamin-mineral requirements are not as great as are those of kittens and mother cats.

Q: My cat loves certain foods and will refuse all others when these are around. Does this mean that these foods are particularly good for him?

A. These are called foods of high acceptability. Most cats, given the opportunity, will settle on a particular food which they will crave to the exclusion of all others. Such foods of high acceptability are usually *not* nutritionally adequate over an extended period. This is exactly similar to a child's craving for a diet of candy and ice cream. Although both are all right as *parts* of a diet, they would certainly cause deficiencies if the child were to be fed nothing else.

Q: What should one feed a pregnant or a nursing cat?

A: To begin, one cannot overfeed a pregnant or lactating cat. She needs two to four times the amount you would feed otherwise. She also needs additional calcium, vitamins and minerals. (She has a special need for vitamin A and the minerals calcium and iodine.) She should be fed raw meat, egg yolks, cooked vegetables and vitamins. You should also know that if a cat becomes pregnant on her first heat (about five to six months of age), she will never grow and develop, since all the nutrients she herself requires for growth will be passed to the gestating kittens. Therefore, do not let your cat breed on the first heat.

Q: Is it wrong to feed vegetables to a cat?

A: Vegetables are not necessary components in a cat's diet, and are indigestible if not cooked. They are all right in limited quantities if the cat eats them voluntarily, but they *must* be cooked.

Q: Is it true that cats get bladder-stone problems from certain foods such as tunafish?

A: Although many veterinarians suspect there is a connection, no experimental relationship has yet been proved. Some researchers feel that high ash diets contribute to the condition. Others think that the main culprits are lack of drinking water and the cat's holding his urine over a long period. Lack of vitamin A has been incriminated also.

Q: How can I work out my cat's caloric needs, that is, the minimum number of calories he needs per day?

A: This is difficult for the average owner. A cat's requirements vary with age, activity and size. For example, an "average" ten-pound male or female needs about 300 calories per day. Growing cats (up to twelve months old) require much higher caloric intakes. A six-month-old male, for instance, may require six to eight hundred, and a young mother cat as many as a thousand calories a day. The easiest way to answer this question for the average owner is to feed the cat as much as he or she will eat twice a day, then start cutting back on these amounts if the cat starts to get fat.

Q: Why do cats eat grass?

A: We don't really know the full answer. We suspect it is due to a nutritional deficiency which the cat is trying to balance by instinct. It is also thought that the cat does this to induce vomiting to rid the stomach of some irritation such as a hairball. The latter theory is upheld by the frequent observation that cats with worms commonly eat grass.

Q: My cat catches birds, mice and an occasional lizard. Is this bad for him?

A: As we have already discussed, cats living in the wild subsist on this kind of prey. However, in the urban environment, many of these rodents and birds die from poisoning. Cats who eat them may become ill. In addition, rodents carry the intermediate stage of various tapeworms, and can infect the cat who eats their carcasses. Some lizards are poisonous to cats, and the skins of lizards may cause severe indigestion. Intestinal obstruction may come from the undigested bones of these small creatures. The cat may also get a bacterial infection from wild prey, either from eating an animal with an infection, or from eating one which had decomposed. Rabies can be transmitted by a bite inflicted on the cat by prey in the course of struggle.

Another common problem of cats is eating grasshoppers, flies and assorted insects killed by insecticides. Cats are very susceptible to small doses of these common poisons.

These hazards of the hunting cat are listed as reasons for discouraging your cat from eating wild prey whenever you can. We do not intend to alarm cat owners, since these problems come up only occasionally.

Q: What are the best natural sources of essential vitamins and minerals most commonly deficient in cats?

A: Vitamin A: fish oils, eggs, raw liver; vitamin D: fish oils, irradiated yeast, butter; vitamin E: wheat germ oil; thiamine: raw liver; riboflavin: raw liver; niacin: raw liver; pyridoxine: raw liver; calcium: bones, milk, cottage cheese; phosphorus: meat; iron: raw liver; copper: raw liver; iodine: enough in commercial foods or table scraps.

*NOTE—These references to moist (canned) and dry (packaged) foods are used only as examples of what total weights of food may be fed your cat daily. They do *not* mean that you should feed all canned food or all dry food. They can generally be taken to mean that these are the totals of varied foods you would feed in a day.

Anna P. Gilbride, D.V.M.

Chapter 17

YOUR CAT'S ENVIRONMENT

Cat, if you go outside you must walk in the snow
You will come back with little white shoes on your feet,
Little white slippers of snow that have heels of sleet.
Stay by the fire, my Cat. Lie still, do not go.

Elizabeth J. Coatsworth (1893)

A good place to live means everything to a cat. Since he has made his home with us for some centuries, he appreciates the same kinds of comfort we do.

The cat who is allowed the run of the house is happier and healthier than the cat who is too closely confined. But complete freedom in a neighborhood full of dangers may mean injury and death.

Parents who allow their children to run loose in the streets may run afoul of the law and invite tragedy. People who allow their cats to run freely are, to an extent, guilty of the same offense. Allowing our cats such random freedom not only jeopardizes their health and safety, but helps cat haters (ailurophobes) to howl all the more against them.

If a family has one, two, or even four cats, it is entirely possible to give them the run of the house without too much encroachment on family living. When the number exceeds this, the walk-in cage becomes a necessity.

The Walk-In Cage

The walk-in cage should be so constructed and of such size, not less than four feet by six feet by eight feet high, that several cats can move about, jump on shelves of varying heights, walk around catwalks halfway up and two-thirds of the way up to the ceiling with several resting shelves at various distances from the floor. The walk-in cage should be completely furnished with cat furniture, such as cat trees, baskets, box houses, rugs, and toys.

A cat in captivity needs his owner's attention. A home with too many cats will deprive him of this personal touch. Too many cats also put a burden on the owner. In order for a cat to be healthy, strong and fun-loving, he must have clean and tidy quarters, must be groomed daily and allowed daily exercise. With all this the extra, "Hello, I'm here with you," is mandatory for him.

The care of four cats is time-consuming, the good care

of more is a full-time job. If the owner has no helpers to do the menial chores, how can he experience and enjoy the complete personality of each loved cat?

When Patti O'Hern, Executive Secretary of Pet Pride, moved to her new home in Thousand Oaks, she chose the largest room in the house with cross ventilation (approximately thirty by twenty feet) for a home for her nine cats.

She had individual walk-in chalets, four by four by eight feet of expanded metal, built in on one side of the room. This provides sleeping and eating room for individual cats. Most of the time the cats live in the open part of the room which is furnished with sofa, chairs, tables and regular cat furniture.

One of the interesting things about this cat home is the sliding glass windows over the sink area in the kitchen. Patti can watch her cats companionably as she prepares their food, washes dishes and so forth.

On the other side of the room are floor-to-ceiling glass doors which open on the garden and swimming pool. This gives the cats a chance to watch all her activities. They like being part of things.

Nothing is so boring as to be shut away in a room without a view or anything to watch or participate in. Cats need entertainment as well as we.

A West Virginia couple wrote Pet Pride explaining that their cats are kept in their own home.

"Our cats have their own special rooms to play in and sunny windows where they may sun themselves.

"In our well-constructed basement, we have provided scratching posts, shelves, beds and toys. All these keep them comfortable and amused if they must be shut up for a time. We have no specifically built cages. However, we keep one cage for an emergency illness and, of course, have our carriers.

"Our cats are groomed daily. We always check on the flea situation. If necessary, powder or spray from our veterinarian is used. We also have our cats checked by the veterinarian every six months.

"Their dishes are washed and rinsed thoroughly. The litter pans are changed daily and scrubbed with hot water and a clear soap.

"With all this attention, they are healthy and happy."

A Cattery

If you are breeding cats, things become more complicated. Sylvia Moberly Holland describes her cattery as follows:

If one could have the ideal cattery, everything exactly as it should be, it would be wonderful. But this would be a full-time job, and not many people can afford it for the simple reason that a cattery is not income producing. Most of us have to cope with a bread-and-butter job, and perhaps a second job as housekeeper as well. The cats have to be job number three.

"But what is all this hard work?" one may ask. "I have several cats at home—just stray cats, you know, but I love them—and they are no trouble all."

To begin with, in a cattery, one has male stud cats and unspayed females who come in season all too regularly. One has to cope with their moods of passion and rage, with the sweet little females who turn into screaming furies when love is in the air, with boisterous males all set to eliminate potential competition.

Item two—cages and runs and reliable helpers whose price is above rubies. Cages and runs mean building, painting, repairing, sweeping, cleaning, twice-daily changing of litter boxes and checking of beds, preparing of food, washing dishes—and ordering (and paying for) supplies.

Illness? This is bad enough when you have one or

two cats. In a cattery illness may spread until the owner is a wreck and the veterinarian's bill astronomical. Some of the babies may die—and few things in the world are sadder than a dying kitten.

This sounds depressing, but there are many hours of fun, too. The secret is to organize the cattery as simply as possible. We use paper cartons for beds— free and disposable when dirty or chewed on. Litter boxes are plastic dish pans, scrubbed daily with a long-handled brush dipped in disinfectant (not phenol). Water and food dishes are washed daily with detergent and hot water and rinsed in disinfectant solution.

Chopped raw horsemeat is delivered in fifty-pound lots and kept in the freezer in one-pound packages, defrosted as needed. Canned cat food is delivered by the case. Every day half-meat and half-canned food is mixed in two big bowls, with vitamin powder added. Each cat is served twice a day in an individual dish. We add a few pieces of dry cat food on top—different flavors—for chewing.

Our place is on a hillside in Southern California, with no traffic. Our cats can run on the grass and climb trees all year round; though the stud cats and females in season have to take turns under supervision. They do not run away. This is their home and they like it. But we pay a penalty in that they can— and do—catch all the unwelcome pests that stray over our hillside. Cats who live indoors are generally safer and easier to care for.

At suppertime everybody comes in. The cage doors are shuttered. There might be coyotes outside, we tell our tenants. In summer we run sprinklers over the cages. One year the thermometer read 116° F in the shade and all the cats had their mouths open, panting like dogs. We filled a washtub with cold water and dipped each cat, holding him or her by all four feet. They did not mind, and stopped panting. In winter we have little 12-volt heaters, on a special transformer, in each cage. These heaters are set in perforated metal boxes so the cats cannot reach them. We do not recommend this unless you happen to have a tame family electrician. We have one.

This may sound easy, but is like a farm in that someone has to be there, day in and day out, year in and year out.

When we have illness we do all the nursing we can at home, but we cannot do without our veterinarian for anything serious. Notice if a cat is refusing food or water, or has a runny nose or eyes. Watch the elimination. Check for worms, fleas, earmites, hidden abscesses or dried dirt in the fur that might attract flies.

ADMINISTERING PILLS. Often the veterinarian prescribes pills and medicines which the owner pays for and takes home with him but which never get into the cat. We sympathize! It is a tough job to open a cat's mouth and see that a pill or a dose gets down his bitterly resisting throat.

We use the "mummy-wrap"—holding his front paws down and rolling him up so tight in a big thick towel that he cannot get any feet out, and then getting a courageous helper to hold his head still, hand over the ears. Keep your hand out of reach of his teeth. Cutting the sharp tips off his claws with a nail clipper before treating him helps.

NEWBORN KITTENS. Fortunately cats usually get well by themselves. But kittens need watching. We have learned to look for two things when kittens are first born. Pick them up carefully with very clean hands to make sure that the umbilical cords are cut and that the kitten is freed from the mother and the placenta. If the mother doesn't do this, cut the cord with clean scissors not less than 1-¼" from the kitten's body, and pinch it tight to stop any bleeding. Make sure that no cord is wound around any part of the kitten. The cords dry and shrink quickly, and can cut off the circulation from a tiny limb, with disastrous results.

Avoid giving newborn kittens a terry-cloth or fluffy wool blanket for a bed. Claws can catch in this kind of fabric. A cotton sheet or baby blanket are good so long as mother does not claw it up and lose the kittens under it.

Kittens' eyes should open in a week to nine days, clean and clear; if the eyes remain shut, look swollen, with granulation along the lids, bathe them open promptly with warm water on cotton.

Keep them off the floor and the ground, where germs come from people's shoes. Keep up with the vitamins. Feed them often once they have started to eat (at four to five weeks), even if you are very busy. Beware of diarrhea (they can dehydrate very quickly) and keep a sharp eye on their little behinds. If the mother does not keep them spotlessly clean, do it for her. Act promptly for sniffles or running eyes.

With normal luck all will go well, and you and their mother will have a ball watching over an enchanting nestful.

BREEDING. Before we can expect kittens, we must have a love affair, so here comes a word about the bride and groom. Most adult males simply cannot stand each other and they can fight to kill. So one must figure out who should be neutered, and whether one has enough room for adequate separate runs.

We have double breeding cages with a movable wire partition between them. The male goes in on one side, the female on the other. They can measure each other's state of emotion through the wire before actually being in touch. We have learned to be careful of two things. If a male is put into a cage recently occupied by another male, he will smell him and may think the shrinking virgin on the other side of the wire is a rival. He will arch his neck and howl and bristle. He might attack the female. The same thing might happen if the female has been with another male. So make sure that your young male knows that the sweet little furry object on the other side of the wire is a female before you pull the slide. It may take no time at all, or much longer.

Some young females are terribly coy. They want to play or hide under the bedclothes when approached with amorous intent. They keep rolling over instead of posing properly, chin down and rear end up. They may have to be held.

Sometimes we have a female who prefers the role of the lily of purity whose virtue is being assailed. She will get behind anything she can and show only her flattened ears and furious eyes. If her lover comes near, she will poke him right in the face. But give her time and look close—her claws are not out. Pay no attention to her hideous growling and snarling—it is all part of the fun. A ghastly scream usually signals that the deed is done. Boy is sitting on the shelf—well out of reach—with a stunned expression on his face, while Girl is rolling madly about, spitting and striking at everything within reach. Ah, Romance!

"Well, that's that," smiles the owner and reaches for the calendar to mark the first day that the kittens may be expected—sixty-three days from now. The matings may go on for several days. More than one should certainly be allowed.

Sometimes a strange cat coming into a cattery to be mated is so upset by the contrast between her perfumed satin pillows and loving subjects at home and the bare cage into which she has been thrust that she goes right out of season—no matter how mad for love she was a few minutes before. "I am not used to sleeping in a barn!" she cries and will have nothing whatever to do with the big smelly oaf leering at her through the wire. She may come around and coyly try to attract his attention in a day or two. Or she may not, in which case she must be taken home—perhaps to try again another time.

These love affairs may be carried on in the home if there is no breeding cage, but beware—the male will spray all around to attract his lady love, and so, perhaps, will she. So make the honeymoon cottage the bathroom or the back porch, which can be easily cleaned afterward. Their idea of delicious perfume is not quite the same as ours.

MANNERS. "Cat manners" is a consideration we have found almost as important as health in raising kittens. A kitten who is going to live with people must learn quite a number of things that he wouldn't have to know if he were a baby wildcat. He comes into the world all ready to be one of the gang; to purr and play and eat and be petted; but there is more than one way of doing some of these things.

If mother cat is a gracious well-behaved Establishment housecat, she will set up a kittengarten for her brood. She will show them where the litter box is—and clean up after them with a rather concerned expression on her face. She will teach them, by example, not to jump on the table or the stove and how to negotiate the screen door. But if she is a cattery cat, she cannot teach them about rooms and furniture and the noise of the vacuum cleaner—and the big but harmless family dog. They will have to learn those things by themselves when they go to their new homes. This will take a little time and patience on the part of the new owner.

Perhaps—and we hope not—mother cat herself is a non-conformist, hippie housecat who will do too good a job of showing her little dears how to snatch food off the table, climb the drapes and do high-wire stunts on the curtain rods. In fact, she will even nod with approval when the kitten shreds the upholstery. Kittens *can* be taught not to do these things, but if one did not succeed in teaching the mother, what can one expect from the children? For the sake of the cattery kitten's future, begin its training in manners early.

INOCULATIONS. At eight weeks they are ready to embark on the next stage of their life—teenagers! Inoculations for baby diseases, but most of all for the dreaded killer, feline enteritis, and pneumonitis.

We try to bring them into the house at this age, to "walk" them, as is done with foxhound puppies who are soon to join the pack. Each kitten is different. We watch to see who dominates and who loses out in the pecking order. We teach them to eat out of separate plates; to be picked up graciously without spitting in the picker-upper's face; not to bite or scratch even in play. We talk to them and love them every moment we can. This is a must.

BUYING A CAT. Now is the time when people will come to buy them. And while we are watching the kittens' manners we watch the people too.

Visiting a cattery should be a delightful experience for both the owner and visitor. However, there are rules to be acknowledged. The rules are simple, everyday good manners:

Please telephone or write to make an appointment, and come at the appointed time or phone to postpone the visit. Please don't keep the cattery owner waiting for you. A cattery is not quite the same as a pet shop.

If you bring your cat or dog with you, please keep him in the car. He may cause an uproar in the cattery.

Please do not bring in a sick animal. Cattery owners are mortally afraid of germs.

Please do not visit if you have a sick cat at home. Above all, please do not come with the sad news that your cat died yesterday of an infectious illness and you want a kitten right away to replace him. The owner will be glad to help, but wait twenty-one days before introducing a new kitten into the home.

If your cat—alas! has just been run over, do not be surprised if the cattery owner hesitates about letting you have another unless you can give assurance that this will not happen again.

Please do not think that if you bargain smartly you can acquire a $100 show kitten for $25. This is embarrassing for the owner, and it really does cost that much to raise one. If money is a problem, there are many lovely free cats in the shelters, all longing for a home.

By all means bring your children and friends. Cattery owners look forward to your visits and many fine friendships start this way. But please do not let your children rush about shouting and chasing the kittens. This frightens the cats out of their wits.

When you take home a kitten, remember that loud voices and rough handling, however kindly meant, exhaust kittens. Let him have plenty of quiet time to thoroughly explore his new surroundings—and plenty of sleep. A friendly gentle kitten can become quite growly if handled incessantly. We would be unhappy to see this happen to any kitten.

The cattery owner wants you to be delighted with your kitten and will cooperate with you one hundred per cent. But please don't regard him as your ever-available cat doctor forever afterwards. He will do his best. But have a heart—he is a busy person.

And please, above all, don't think that if weeks, months or years later you do not want to keep your cat you have the *right* to hand her back to the cattery where you bought her. It is true that most cattery owners would want to know if a cat of theirs is being "dumped" but she is your cat now—the responsibility is yours.

And please, above all, don't think that if months or years later you do not want to keep your cat that you have the *right* to hand her back to the cattery where you bought her. It is true that most cattery owners would want to know if a cat of theirs is being "dumped" but she is your cat now—the responsibility is yours.

The Shelter

Another kind of cat environment is the shelter. Pet Pride does not advocate any plan for cats' housing which simply includes long rows of compartments without a view, without the possibility of their seeing human activity, without areas for play and exercise. A cat who receives no human attention and companionship is a bored, unhappy cat. An orphanage or cattery that does not consider the emotional health of its cats is not doing its job.

Any group planning to build a cat shelter should make sure it is designed with the deepest concern for the comfort and health of the cats. The one pictured here is an approximate square with all cats in walk-in compartments fully furnished with cat furniture, including cat trees.

Note the plan for ease of operation, with the pick-up, delivery, and storage areas, the well-equipped kitchen for food preparation and the washer and dryer for cat bedding, the Grooming Room through which every cat must pass before entering the shelter proper. The large Nursery

50'-0"

150'-0"

PROP. LINE

OUTDOOR AREA

NURSERY

CAGE 6x8

CAGE 6x8

CAGE 6x7

CAGE 6x6

CAGE 7x9

CAGE 4x4

CAGE 4x4

CAGE 6x4

CAGE 6x4

CAGE 4x4

CAGE 4x4

CAGE 6x4

CAGE 6x4

CAGE 4x4

GROOMING

CORRIDOR

CORRIDOR

ATRIUM OPEN TO SKY

TABLE

D.

KITCH.

F

W

D

STORAGE

SAND

TRASH

MULTI-PURPOSE ROOM

C.

WC M

WC W

VESTIBULE

ENTRANCE

STAIRS

OFFICE

CLINIC

C C

CARETAKER

BATH

CARETAKER II

PICK-UP/DELIVERY

5'-0"

would house the mother and babies in sanitary peace and comfort. The small Clinic will serve as a check-in station for every abandoned cat. Neutering and spaying would be conducted here—our greatest need today if we are to gain control of our overpopulation. The Multi-Purpose Room not only would serve as a lounging room for cats but would have many other important uses.

The Office is conveniently located and would be decorated with an aim of inspiring the visitor to take good care of his adopted cat. Note that the caretaking cat people would be living with the cats, sharing their kitchen and living room, just as in a smaller family home. This is planned particularly to give company to the cats. Many of our shelter cats cry out for attention and companionship, not for food. This shelter, in spite of its ability to house a hundred cats, is really a simulated home. It should always be run by people who sincerely love cats and will make their lives worth living.

Our underlying philosophy is to unite Cat People to put forth every effort to make the cat so popular, so beloved, so sought after, so enjoyed and appreciated that no one will dare abuse him, belittle him, experiment on his body (save for his own sake), or refrain from caring for him. In order to make a cat popular, he must be clean, free of disease and parasites, and of good disposition. A shelter is an ideal place to show off the cat as he should be kept in ideal surroundings. As the public begins to understand the basic needs of cats, both physical and emotional, so then will cats be helped.

Chapter 18

CARING FOR CATS

Here are the answers to some common questions asked about caring for cats.

Q: What kind of collars should be used for a cat?

A: It is not necessary to use collars if cats are properly protected inside or outside in a cat-proof area. Letting cats run loose is one of the serious problems that the American people must solve. Collars are sometimes very dangerous to cats; sometimes they can get their jaws caught, causing serious head injury, or they can get caught on some obstruction and hang themselves to death. If you must use a collar, use an elastic one that is *not* tight; elastic collars for cats are usually sold in pet stores.

Q: Should I put a bell on my cat?

A: Never put a bell around your cat's neck. The constant ringing every time the cat moves can seriously affect the cat's emotional stability.

Q: How do you pick up a cat?

A: Never pick up a cat by the loose skin around its neck; this can seriously injure a grown cat who weighs several pounds. A cat should be picked up with one hand under his stomach and chest. This gives the cat the support he needs without any strain on his organs.

Q: What is the best carrier for the cat?

A: There are several good carriers on the market. They can be made of wood, leather, plastic or metal and should be well-ventilated. A carrier should be big enough for a grown cat to rest comfortably. It should also be strong; a weak, poorly made carrier is of no use—either the carrier will collapse in an emergency situation or the cat will be able to escape and be lost. If traveling for more than a couple of hours, a carrier should be big enough to contain a litter pan.

Q: What is the best way to travel long distances with a cat?

A: They should always be in a carrier, of course. Don't feed your cat anything for at least four hours before starting, and don't feed the cat at all during the journey unless it is more than twenty-four hours. Be sure to give the cat fresh water every few hours. Try not to open the carrier at any time; your cat may panic and escape. Don't bother the cat too much; it only upsets him. Speak to your cat in a soothing tone. Try to keep your cat with you, not in a baggage compartment. Never ship your cat alone; too many things can go wrong when the cat and carrier are not supervised by someone who cares. In general, cats do not like to travel. They like familiar surroundings. It is better to board your cat than subject him to frightening experiences.

Q: Where should I board my cat?

A: No cat should be left at a boarding place that is not recommended by a reliable person or approved by an organization such as Pet Pride. Minimum requirements should be: a separate cage for your cat, cleanliness of surroundings, a proper diet and fresh water.

Q: What is the best bedding for a cat?

A: Clean flannel blankets—the kind used for babies—are good bedding.

Q: How much sleep do cats require?

A: Cats sleep the number of hours that are right for them. Much depends on their owners' sleeping habits and how long they are left alone.

Q: How do I keep my cat from scratching the furniture?

A: Keep your cat's claws clipped with a nail clipper. The claws are like fingernails and the bloodline shows clearly. The tips, below the bloodline, may be clipped off without harm or pain to the cat. Have your veterinarian show you how to clip the cat's claws. If you provide a scratching post, made of carpet or cork, and teach the cat how to use it, it will save your furniture. This training should begin when your cat is a kitten, for it is easier then.

Q: How can a cat be toilet-trained for the litter box?

A: Most cats are trained by their mothers when they are four to six weeks of age. Whenever you bring a cat into a new place, show him where the litter box is. Cats naturally want to cover this evidence of their presence, and commercial litter is best for this need and is available in all markets. You should clean the litter box regularly and replace the litter. Wash the box (plastic or metal) with a mild soap.

Chapter 19

WARNING—DANGEROUS FOR CATS

Chemicals

Any product containing phenol is extremely dangerous to cats. As little as four drops of pure phenol can kill a grown cat. Even licking phenol liquids off their feet can make cats very ill. Phenol is used in many household cleansers and sanitizing products, so check your cabinets. Lysol, for example, in both liquid and spray form, is toxic to cats. Simply spraying it in the air around a cat can cause eye irritation and upset stomachs. Walking in the wet spray can kill them.

Paints with a lead base are poisonous to a cat. Cats are also sensitive to chlorinated hydrocarbons, such as are found in cleaning fluids, some spray paints and other spray products. Inhaling the spray can cause serious lung and liver problems. These products have a similar effect on humans, but the cat is so much smaller that a proportionately small amount will cause poisoning.

If you plan to use a spray paint, to spray for insects, to spray your yard, or even wax your floor, take a moment and be sure your cat is safely confined—and keep him that way until all moisture and odor have disappeared. Clorox and ammonia-type cleansers are generally not poisonous to cats unless, of course, the cats try to lap them up (but let's hope they are smart enough not to).

Fleas

One never-ending problem to Cat People and their cats is the flea. Keeping your cat indoors will help immensely, but it's possible to bring fleas inside on your shoes. If in combing your cat you notice a fine pepper-like matter on the skin, you have or have had fleas. Always use a fine-toothed flea comb for testing.

Another word of warning, though—many cats are made ill by the use of the wrong flea powder. Most flea powders are made for dogs and are poisonous to cats. Never use a flea powder that does not specifically say on the label "Safe For Cats." Better yet, obtain flea powder from your veterinarian who may have one not available in a pet shop. The most effective flea powder contains nepthyl-n-methylcarbamate. Any powder containing DDT, chlordane or lindane is poisonous to cats. Rotenone or pyrethrum are less dangerous but are still not as safe as the n-methylcarbamate types.

The best way to apply flea powder is to rub it on the skin under the hair on top of the head, across the shoulders and down the backbone. This will kill the fleas without the cat's being able to reach it or lick off. Remember to dust the cat's bedding, too, and the corners where he sleeps. Fleas have a life cycle of several weeks, so don't expect to be rid of them with one treatment. Continue using flea powder several times a week, for two or three weeks. Then for prevention, use it once a week.

Mites

At least once a week check your cat's ears and clean the ears if necessary. Cats try very hard to be clean, but the inside of the ear is one place they can't manage without human help. The best way to do this is to dip a cotton swab in alcohol or mineral oil and swab out the canal. If a dark, crusty type wax is noted that doesn't respond to regular cleaning, probably ear mites are present. They can be easily treated if caught early. If ignored, they will cause a secondary infection that can become extremely serious. Several ear drops are available that will cure the condition. Your veterinarian will recommend something to keep on hand. Use according to his direction. If the cat scratches at his ears a good deal, suspect ear mites, even if you don't notice any waxy discharge.

Eye Infections

Occasionally cats will develop a mild eye infection or eye allergy. If you notice your cat has matter in the corner of his eyes, wipe them out daily and apply a mild human-type opthalmic antibiotic for several days—it will generally work. However, if there is any pain, or the eye looks inflamed, check at once for foreign matter. Cats often get a bit of litter in their eyes. You must remove it in exactly the same way as you would from a human eye.

Worms

Roundworms and tapeworms are both common in cats. Tapeworms are usually found if the cat has fleas. Roundworms tend to give the cat a small, dry cough, hurt his appetite and cause him not to feel well. Tapeworms can be detected in the cat's stool or as small dry grains in his bed or on his coat. Home worming is not a good idea with cats—if the medication is not harmful, it will be ineffective and if effective, it may kill the cat.

Pneumonitis

Pneumonitis is a cat disease similar to a cold or influenza in humans. The main symptoms are runny nose, sneezing, red and weepy eyes. Pneumonitis itself is curable in adult cats but serious with small kittens. The nose problem will interfere with your cat's desire to eat. If he can't smell his food, he will not eat it. This lack of appetite is the major problem in pneumonitis. You must forcefeed food of high caloric value. Baby foods are good for this. If you suspect your cat has pneumonitis, treat him quickly before he stops eating. Check with your veterinarian on the advisability of giving tylocine and some type of antihistamine. These have been found helpful in drying up the cat's nose so that he will eat. While there are serums on the market for pneumonitis, they are not entirely satisfactory—just as influenza shots for humans do not inoculate against all strains of the disease, and last only a short time. The best prevention is to avoid being around or handling other cats who have symptoms of influenza.

Rabies

Although many people worry about rabies, it is extremely rare in cats—so rare that many veterinarians have never treated a case. While it is entirely possible for a rabid dog to transmit the disease to a cat, rabies can be transmitted only by the bite of an infected animal. Unless you hear of a case in the neighborhood, this disease need not be worried about.

Abcesses

Cats who are allowed outside are prone to abscesses, something almost unheard-of in a housecat. In a fight, the cat will acquire many deep tiny puncture wounds from the other cat's claws. These will heal almost at once, but three to five days later an abscess will form under the skin. If it is fairly near the surface, you will be able to feel it and take some action.

Unfortunately many of these wounds are so deep that your first hint of trouble will be a sick cat, with a high fever and other symptoms you would expect with a serious infection. Prompt veterinary treatment is essential for anything but the most superficial abscesses. A true Cat Person will keep his pet indoors and avoid the problem entirely.

Although cats are subject to many of the same problems humans know, such as heart trouble, tumors, cancer, arthritis and kidney stones, the well-cared-for cat can live to fifteen or more years in a house. Ten to twelve is quite common. The cat allowed to run loose rarely survives too long—he just isn't capable of outrunning cars any more.

Teeth

If your cat shows signs of a sore mouth, or doesn't want to chew his food, check his teeth. Cats are subject to tartar formation, especially on the back teeth. This presses on the gums, is very painful and will keep your cat from eating, which is always dangerous. Removing the tartar is a job for your veterinarian but it can be prevented to some extent by encouraging your cat to chew hard, crunchy dry cat foods. I frequently sprinkle a few of these on their regular meals.

Cystitis

Cystitis is a common disorder of mature cats and is especially noted in males. It is an inflammation of the bladder and can lead to the formation of small stones. These stones cause him pain on urination and can cause blockage. If this occurs, the cat will die within a short time.

The symptoms are easy to detect. If your cat goes to his litter box often but doesn't accomplish anything, don't assume he is constipated, assume he has cystitis. If you pick him up under his stomach and he cries, watch him for these symptoms. Cystitis can be treated fairly easily if caught early, but blockage is very difficult to treat. Although the exact cause of cystitis is not known, it is known to be more common in males than in females. Cats should not be altered until fully grown. Cystitis is found more often in cats altered from five to eight months than in those altered later. Fish diets seem to have some part in causing cat cystitis in spite of the ads which declare that they are nutritionally complete. It is wise to feed a varied diet, including fresh raw meat. If cystitis develops, feed a diet high in Vitamin A and low in ash and calcium.

Hairballs

Hairballs are particularly a problem of Persians and other longhairs. Only occasionally will a shorthair swallow enough hair to cause trouble. Every few days give your shorthair a good combing with a small, fine-toothed steel comb. Finish the grooming by wiping his coat down with a rough, slightly damp washcloth. A washcloth dipped in Listerine is also good to use.

It is absolutely essential that a long-haired cat be combed regularly. It is impossible for the cat to rid himself of the long loose hair, especially in spring and summer, when normal shedding occurs. This loose hair will cause two serious problems if not combed out regularly. The first is hairballs from hair that the cat swallows; the second is matting from the dead hair left on the cat. Both conditions are serious. Occasionally cats will spit up the matted hair without help, but if you suspect hairball, treat it at once. Use Petromalt or Gerimalt—your cats are usually willing to eat this and it will prove satisfactory. Bacon fat or salad oil are also generally effective.

As a matter of practice, if your cat spends any time at all licking his coat, be scrupulous about combing out loose hair—this is the only good solution to the hairball problem.

Matting

Matting is a health problem as well as a grooming problem. If the mats are noted early, they are easy to remove. If they are not removed, the cat can quickly develop mats so serious that it becomes necessary to place him under anesthesia and shave him to take care of the problem. Matting is the single most common problem that the longhair breeder faces, yet the easiest to prevent. Daily combing in spring and summer, and combing at least once a week the rest of the year, will solve the problem. Many Cat People do not believe that brushing alone will help. They say this merely covers up the beginning mats and leaves a frill of pretty brushed hair. They recommend using an imported steel comb with long widely spaced teeth and combing firmly from head to tail, right down to the skin. Be especially sure to check the spots where the mats first form—just behind the ears, between the front legs on the chest, between the hind legs on the stomach, on the backs of the hind legs, behind the knee joint, and on the bottoms of the feet. A female cat nursing her babies will often develop mats over the hips and on the shoulders.

If you discover a small mat, try to separate it with the comb. If it won't separate easily, give it a sharp pull, holding the skin with the other hand, and see if it will simply pull out. If this won't work, use the scissors and cut it out. Don't worry about leaving a hairless spot—the Persian coat grows rapidly and cutting out matted hair is far better than leaving even one tiny mat to start more trouble. Many fanciers clip their cats in the early spring. This not only makes it easier to care for them during the shedding season, but the coat that comes in the fall will be heavier and longer and healthier in many cases. If you do clip your Persian, clip only the sides, back and stomach to about an inch. Leave the tail, the ruff around the neck and the hair on the backs of the legs, as the hair here grows more slowly than the body hair.

Swallowing Obstructions

As a final warning, for your cat's sake be careful to provide an environment that does not allow him to play with or swallow any of the following: rubber bands, cellophane or plastic wrappings from cigarettes or laundry, string, cotton cord, thread, wool of any kind, electric cords, bamboo from curtains or straws from brooms. Many kittens die each year from swallowing these things. Usually by the time they are grown they have better sense, but even as adults they are better off with your eye on their activities.

Poisons

Provide an environment that does not permit your cat to suffer from other animal poisons, including snakes, lizards and insects. Avoid plants and mushrooms containing toxic substances such as philodendron, holly berries, poinsettia leaves and stems, rhododendron, laurel, mistletoe, calla lily and chrysanthemum.

Always be alert to the dangers that your cat may confront. Try to understand that his curiosity may sometimes lead him into danger. Remember that he is entirely dependent upon you and your carelessness could unwittingly cause his illness and death. Your veterinarian is your best friend. Have his number always at hand for any emergency. To receive prompt medical attention when necessary is one of the benefits that the lucky cat should enjoy.

Pat Robie

Chapter 20

THE DISEASE WE FEAR MOST

Many of us who were breeding cats in the thirties remember that just about any or all illnesses were classified as feline distemper, especially if the cat had a temperature, nasal or oral discharge and sneezed. The word "distemper" included respiratory and intestinal disorders. Any other disorder with similar or varying symptoms was diagnosed as "atypical distemper."

Now we know that rhinitis, sinusitis, conjunctivitis and influenza are different from the intestinal diseases. They are now classed as respiratory diseases, rather than being included in the distemper group.

And today we know that the virus which British scientists isolated and associated with infectious enteritis, and the virus causing panleukopenia which was isolated by American scientists, are one and the same. The British concentrated on the intestinal symptoms while the Americans concentrated on the changes in the blood. As a result, a vaccine called feline distemper vaccine was developed to protect our cats from this serious and contagious disease. Although the disease is now called panleukopenia, the vaccine used against it is still called feline distemper vaccine—such is life.

Panleukopenia (feline infectious enteritis) is an especially contagious disease and the fatality rate is extremely high. To kittens it is lethal. The virus is transmitted by nasal discharge, food, infected feces or fleas. Its virulence is so great that it can be fatal three to six days from the first appearance of symptoms. In most instances, by the time symptoms are noticed, it is too late to save the cat.

Symptoms vary little—high temperature, lack of appetite, possibly a nasal or eye discharge, emesis (yellow fluid), some diarrhea, desire for water but inability to drink, attitude weak and unresponsive. The temperature may rise to, or above, 105 degrees, hold there for thirty-six to forty hours and then begin to drop. It will rise again in an irregular pattern. This virus works in two stages (proven in laboratories) but usually the cat is in the second stage before symptoms are noticed and treatment begins. In some cases, thanks to new and excellent antibiotics, the second stage (erratic temperature) is better controlled and the much-weakened cats will sometimes survive.

An intensive program for inoculation has almost eliminated the disease, but recently, much to the fanciers' dismay, another virus has appeared with similar symptoms, working in the same manner, causing many fatalities to already inoculated cats and kittens. This new virus is as

yet unnamed. Some veterinarians believe it to be the same virus that causes panleukopenia, but a strain that is immune to the trusted feline vaccine, just as we have a strain of mosquito that is immune to DDT sprays.

Those of you whose cats or kittens have died during the immunity period after inoculation, with a veterinarian's report of enteritis, will understand what I mean. However, most present panleukopenia vaccines administered by veterinarians are highly effective. Inoculations must be given to kittens when the immunity once acquired from their mother's milk has disappeared and before they are endangered by exposure to other cats who may spread this virus.

Cats should be given a vaccination for panleukopenia (enteritis) and pneumonitis soon after they are weaned (six or seven weeks). Some veterinarians recommend booster shots later; others do not.

A great many failures in vaccination have been attributed to the lack of a test for when to vaccinate. The New York State Veterinary College has developed such a test in which the degree of immunity can be determined by means of a blood sample. This test will hopefully be available commercially in the near future.

Once again we urge all cat owners to inoculate against feline panleukopenia. You will be happy you did.

Harriet Wolfgang

Chapter 21

YOUR CAT'S HEALTH

Q: What are the signs of a healthy cat and an unhealthy cat?

A: It is very important to watch over your animals and to know whether or not they are feeling well. Feel the cat's ears and nose when he is well; know just how he should look and feel to your touch. Then you will know immediately if there is something wrong by the way he acts, looks, or feels to the touch. Their well-being, freedom from parasites, cleanliness and emotional stability depends on you. Leaving a cat alone for long periods of time without human companionship is inhumane and unkind.

To have a healthy, stable, lovable cat, tender care and treatment of the kitten from birth is important. A kitten should not be subjected to loud, unpleasant noise and confusion, constant rough teasing or sudden disturbances of any kind. Children should not be allowed to handle a cat until they have been taught to do so gently and quietly.

Signs of a healthy cat	Signs of an unhealthy cat
Full of energy	Listlessness
Alert	Dull eyes

Bright eyed	Haws up in the eyes
Shiny coat	Lackluster coat
Good appetite	Coat separates
Playfulness	Coat stands away in sticky
Washes face after eating	manner
Purring	Loss of appetite
Well-formed stools	Pitiful crying
Normal weight	Diarrhea
Has air of poise	Neglects fastidious habits
Contented	Restlessness
Mischievous	Scratches at body
	Shakes head often

At the first sign of an ill cat, you should take him to a veternarian and follow his instructions as to his care. A cat loses ground and dehydrates so rapidly that you must take action at once. A cat who is ill will usually refuse to eat or be very picky about his food. Generally a cat who is not well will be rough in coat. The coat will not lie flat and shiny, but will lack luster and will stand out from the body with a sticky appearance. This is frequently a sign of fever, subnormal temperature or dehydration. The eyes of a sick cat will not be bright and alert. Often the haw, or third eyelid, will come up in the inside corner of the eye until it partially covers the eye. In the case of a cold or pneumonitis, the first symptoms are red, inflamed, or runny eyes.

If it is noticed that the cat goes frequently to his litter pan and strains to urinate with little or no results, it is nearly certain the cat is suffering from bladder stones and must have immediate treatment by your veterinarian or the bladder will burst.

Any persistent vomiting or diarrhea should be noted immediately and you should take the cat to the veterinarian. Sneezing and coughing must be watched carefully. A healthy cat may sneeze or cough occasionally to clear his nose or throat, but persistent symptoms should be treated by a veterinarian.

The presence of worms is very hard on your cat. The worms will deprive the cat of nourishment and will reduce his strength and resistance. Segments of the tapeworm are passed with his bowel movement and are easily seen as small grains resembling rice. The cat may cough up roundworms. Your veterinarian will probably require a fresh specimen of the cat's stool to test for worms, so to save time you should take such a specimen with you when you take the cat for an examination.

Q: What should be done when a cat is suffering from diarrhea?

A: A cat who is suddenly suffering from acute diarrhea should be taken to a veterinarian at once for treatment. If your cat is prone to loose movements and is not an ill animal, then it would be wise to look into in diet. Perhaps he cannot drink milk. Reduce his meat feeding and substitute kibbles for half his meal. Once the stool becomes firmer, then the kibbles can be gradually eliminated. Do not overdo it and end up with a constipated cat, and do not overfeed.

Q: What should be done for a kitten suffering from constipation?

A: A few drops of Karo syrup can be added to his milk.

Q: What should be done for a grown cat's constipation?

A: Temporary constipation caused either by hairballs or overeating can be cleared up with prepared Petromalt or Gerimalt. If a cat has chronic constipation, more milk should be included in his diet and very little bulk, such as canned food or kibbles, should be given to him. In-

crease his raw meat and add a little raw liver or kidney
to his meat feedings.

Q: Can people catch any diseases from cats or vice
versa?

A: According to most scientists, humans cannot catch
diseases from cats. There is a bare possibility, some scientists say, that cats can catch diseases from humans.

Q: What can the cat owner do about rickets?

A: Rickets is a faulty development of the bones due to
defective deposition and utilization of calcium and phos-
porus in a growing kitten. Rickets is caused by inadequate
diet. If the owner improves the diet, it will help the cat.
A veterinarian's advice should be followed.

Q: What can you do for a cat that has "dandruff"?

A: This is usually caused by dry skin and can usually be
cured by including a few drops oil—wheatgerm, corn and
safflower—in the cat's diet.

Q: Can cats get rabies?

A: Yes, but it is extremely rare in cats. Rabies can be
transmitted only by an animal that has the disease. If
your cat is kept away from other animals, there is little
danger of this disease. If you travel with the cat or let
him outdoors, it would be advisable to have him vaccinated.

Q: What kind of care do a cat's teeth need?

A: A cat should be taken once a year to the veterinarian
for the examination and cleaning of teeth. The formation
of tartar on the teeth is the greatest difficulty cats have.

Chapter 22

HOW TO GROOM A LONGHAIRED CAT

It is best for you and your cat if you start grooming him as a kitten—in this way your kitten gets accustomed to regular grooming. It also minimizes tangles and furballs. Daily grooming is best. Use the imported steel combs with long, slim teeth; most good steel combs have both wide-set teeth and finer teeth. A comb with wide-set teeth is used to straighten out tangles and the finer one is used to get out loose hair and the smaller knots. I have also had good luck with a toothbrush for breaking up small tangles that are close to the skin. I apply a generous amount of powder to the tangle first. The gentler you are with your kit the easier it will be for both of you.

Shake baby powder or a mild unperfumed powder into the coat; then run the comb all the way through the fur to the skin. The powder combines with the natural oils and when you comb it or brush it, it separates and aerates the hair, and the kitty's fur becomes very fluffy.

I usually start with the head. I use swabs dipped in warm water to clean the ears first. With another swab, also dipped in warm water, I clean the eyes. I then powder the head lightly, trying to keep the powder away from the nose, eyes and mouth. I use a very fine-toothed comb to comb the short fur on my cats' faces. Pay special attention to the back of the ears and the area between the eyes and the ears. A lot of natural oils show up here. The area near the eyes often gets dark and looks dirty.

Some people think that combing the cat's head, back and tail are enough. It isn't. You must convince kitty from the beginning that the flanks, both front and hind legs, under the chin and chest and the stomach also must be groomed. It is easy to take the short way out, but in the end you and your cat will suffer. My cats are big and my lap is small, so I place them on a large bath towel on my lap and prop up my feet on a foot stool. I follow the same routine for each grooming session. I start at the head and save the tail till the last. The tail also accumulates a lot of body oils and you must work on it faithfully. I powder it and with a flat toothbrush work the powder in well, making sure to remove any black specks that might be on the tail. If a large accumulation of oil is present, dip a cotton swab in Listerine and rub it on the skin.

Some people like to use brushes and some just comb their cats. If you use a brush, be sure it has natural bristles; brush the fur in the opposite direction. Be sure to brush the fur around the ruff to form a frame around your kitty's face.

The more careful you are with your grooming, the less loose fur on your furniture, and what is more important, less fur for kitty to swallow. If you groom every day, you won't need to bathe your kitty as often. Cats are very neat by nature and do not like to be dirty. Our cats are always indoors and we do not have fleas. But an all-over bath is necessary occasionally even if you keep your kitty well groomed.

It takes two people to give kitty a bath. Get together all the things you will need before letting him know what he's in for. You will need two or three bath towels, a wash cloth, kitty's shampoo, a bottle of white vinegar, mineral oil, plastic dropper, and your drying equipment.

If you have a two-sided sink, fill each side half full of warm water before placing your cat in the sink. Or if you have a clown like our Tu Tu, put him in the sink first and let the water run in slowly—Tu Tu plays around in the water.

Start by putting one drop of mineral oil in each eye. When kitty is thoroughly wet, start working the shampoo into his head. If kitty has fleas, they will go to the top of his head and you can pick them off easily. Be sure to wash the skin in front of his ears thoroughly because this is a trouble spot for body oils. Do not be afraid to gently use a small brush or toothbrush to work the oils loose.

Another trouble spot is the tail, which usually has a large amount of oil substance. This is worse on whole cats than on neuters or spays. If you don't get the top of the tail free of oil, the fur will part down the middle and your cat's tail will not look full.

After taking care of the trouble spots, you can shampoo kitty all over. Be sure to work the lather through the fur to the skin.

After he is shampooed all over, and you feel he is clean, be sure to rinse him well. A spray is the best way to rinse the soap off. After all the traces of soap are gone, your kitty may have a cream rinse or a solution of white vinegar diluted in warm clean water (about ¼ cup of vinegar). After this rinse, be sure to rinse with clear water until you are sure all the soap and rinse are out.

Wring out his fur by squeezing it. Place him in a large, dry towel on your lap and be sure to dry his face thoroughly. I use a smaller rough towel to dry him until he lets me know he's had it. If you have a cat cage, place a bath mat on the linoleum; then place the cage over the rug and put your kitty in the cage. If you have a large hair dryer, place it over the cage and the fur will dry quite fast. If the fur can be combed every few minutes, it will help it to dry. If you don't have a hair dryer, place kitty in a very warm room to dry and comb his fur occasionally. Whichever method you use, make sure he is out of the

draft and that he is thoroughly dry before he goes to bed
or is allowed near an open window.

If your cat can take the noise of a small portable hair
dryer, use it on the underside and back of his legs, on his
stomach and his tail. Keep him moving because at this
stage of the game he'll be tired and will want to lie down—
and if the fur is damp, he could catch cold.

A clean kitty usually is a healthy and happy cat.

Elisa Frew

Chapter 23

KITTENS AND HOW THEY GROW

In all of God's great kingdom of creatures divine,
There's none quite so dainty as a kitten so fine.
It does seem a pity that it grows up so soon,
A kitten in the morning and an adult at noon.

Donna Joffrion

Little Emily was bathed and wormed before she was
bred. During the sixty-five days before her confinement
she was served two good meals a day. These included
concentrated high-quality protein and fat (fresh raw beef,
kidney, heart, corn oil, wheat germ oil, yeast powder, hard
cooked eggs, cottage cheese, kelp, alfalfa powder, Pre
Natal Theralin, Abdec Drops and Gerimalt). She had a
good appetite and usually ate her meals. A placid, friendly

cat, she gets along well with the others. She spent the days lounging in the house or in her safe outside area.

Little Emily had one bad habit that worried me. She has always like to squeeze through doors or push herself behind the china closet. Sure enough, a few minutes before her first kitten came, there she was pressed halfway behind this large piece of furniture, slowly making her way inch by inch. I had to take her by the base of the tail and firmly and with force pull her out. What this might do to those babies I didn't know. Had she been left alone at this critical time, her babies might have been born and died before we could have rescued them.

Sunday, April 7. Little Emily was set up in a small room with washable carpet, a box with bedding, water dish, litter tray, sterilized scissors, tissue, a small box with cloth padding for the kittens. The labor period was short—here was the first one, hind feet and legs only. This means a breech birth. I took hold of that little body firmly, trying at the same time to keep Little Emily lying still; as a labor wave seemed to come, I gently but firmly pulled. The baby came—the White One. The placenta came almost at once. I cut it two inches from the body, then pressed the end together. The baby was exhausted and hardly moved. I shook him, holding him with both hands and swung him at arm's length from over my head almost down to the floor, just as I had seen the veterinarian do, wiped his little face, massaged him. He moved weakly. He started to breath. He was going to make it! He was placed in his tiny box, covered up and kept warm. It was an eighty-degree day; no artificial heat was needed.

Little Emily lay back and rested. In about half an hour the little Black Boy came head first. He seemed strong and vigorous. Forty minutes later, the White Girl with the Black Top came along, also head first. All three are now in the small box. Mother is resting. She is taking a little warm milk to drink. There seem to be no more. The two vigorous ones started to nurse immediately. Number One didn't nurse for several hours; he was still too weak and exhausted. I got up in the middle of the night several times to see how they were doing and tried to help Number One to get started nursing. Finally he seemed strong enough. Twice I found he had crawled off to the corner of Little Emily's box. Each time I brought him back to the other two, who were now nursing enthusiastically.

Monday, April 8. All the second day mother and babies rested, nursed and slept. In the early morning I took her to Dr. Pollack for examination and a posterior pituitary injection to be sure all was well. All three were now nursing. Little Emily ate large meals served in bed. I picked up each baby several times a day a minute or two, always with *two* hands. Kittens should always be moved slowly, besides being well supported. They should never learn to fear human hands. We want our kittens relaxed, friendly, confident that they will never be hurt by their Cat People.

Tuesday, April 9. The third day and Little Emily is getting restless. She is dissatisfied with her bed and general environment. She kept picking up the babies and carrying them to a corner of the room. They were crying and objecting. This went on for several hours. Finally, I brought in the portable cage and installed her Three in a cage with her big box, her litter tray, her water and food dishes and a carpeted place to lounge beside her box. She was forced to stay put. They were eating well, growing now and quiet.

Wednesday, April 10. This is Little Emily's fourth day and she wants to get out of her cage. She is let out to walk around. I am careful to close her kittens in so she will not again take a notion to move them. She walks around the house. She visits the cattery and the living room and the kitchen. After a half hour of this she is willing to go back to her contentedly sleeping babies and be locked up in her cage with them.

Saturday, April 13. Little Emily on her seventh day is getting into a routine of walking around the house for a period each day, stretching her legs and using the scratching post. She is content to go back after this and still wants her meals served in bed with her Three. They are in good shape, eating well and growing rapidly. They sleep a great deal of the time.

Sunday, April 14. One week ago today the Three were born. I notice all are the same size; the health of each is excellent, and all are adequately nourished. Little Emily is still content to spend long hours in her box while the babies eat and sleep. Each day they are picked up one at a time, talked to, and made to feel wanted in this world. This is very important.

Tuesday, April 16. On the tenth day they are still easy to care for. The eyes are beginning to open. Now each baby is twice the size of their mother's front paw, which means twice as big as when they were born.

Wednesday, April 17. Now they are very strong babies and are able to crawl around in their mother's box. The eyes are more open but not entirely, especially the two Whites. They look beautiful, healthy, and strong. Little Emily continues to eat well. She has a jar of baby food (concentrated meat) every noon. This extra food is very important to the health of the babies; food should be rich, nourishing, concentrated without too much bulk and very little ash.

Sunday, April 21. On the fifteenth day the eyes of the Black One are more fully open, the White Ones almost.

They crawl a great deal, try to walk, but crumple down frequently. Their size increases rapidly.

Monday, April 22. On the sixteenth day I take them to the photographers for their first professional pictures. Little Emily was out walking around the house. I closed the door to their room so she would not be too worried about their absence. I was only gone about thirty minutes but wanted to avoid having a nursing mother get upset, which, of course, would not be good for the babies.

Monday, April 29. They are three weeks old now. Notice how alert the Black Boy is. He is more precocious than the other two, walks straighter, eyes are more open. He seems more aggressive and stronger. However, he is starting to object to being held. He always squirms more than the others.

April 30 to May 5. Their fourth week and they are starting to get very restless. They want to exercise more and indicate that they would like to crawl over the top of their box. It is too small now and I must think of larger quarters, where they will be protected but have a chance to run, wrestle and play.

May 6. Little Emily's Three are now starting to go into their fifth week. This is considered the cutest age for kittens. I decided to call the first boy White Satin, the second boy Black Satin, and the little White Girl with the black top hair Marlene Dietrich, whom I saw this afternoon give her superb performance. If my Marlene is as beautiful in her way as her namesake is in hers, we'll easily have a future grand champion.

May 11. I moved them into a larger cage (five feet wide, two feet deep, twenty-seven inches high). This I place over a sheet on the carpeted floor. It contains the original box with a door cut in it so the kittens can get out, a low litter pan, and water dish. This longer cage contains two doors which lift up from the floor and are out of the way when one wishes. I spread out a sheet in front of the cage doors. The kittens have easy access from cage to outside area. They are staying on the sheet and mother lies and watches close by.

May 12. White Satin took his first running steps today. The other two are still walking rather slowly. They have plenty of opportunity now to exercise and grow strong and healthy. They still feel like little soft balls, have good short bodies. They are investigating the litter pan but have not used it yet. Little Emily is a good mother. She keeps them clean, watches over them continually and feeds them well. I continue to handle them every day and am combing them, washing their eyes and faces.

May 14 to 17. The fifth week and White Satin is the first to start eating, then little Marlene. I made them a mixture of Esbilac, a substitute for mother's milk, and warm water with Pablum, yeast powder, cottage cheese, yogurt, a few ABDEC Drops and a little Prental Theralin. Black Satin, who was so forward when he was younger, backs away from his flat dish of food and refuses as yet to taste the food. He prefers Little Emily's milk still. The others also nurse occasionally, besides drinking their thick liquid food.

May 20. Six weeks old today. They are eating and nursing both now. Black Satin still backs away from his food when being watched. I have come upon him unexpectedly and found him eating as the others from the large, flat dish of liquid food. White Satin is beginning to taste the solid food prepared for his mother.

May 21 to May 26. During the sixth week the kittens, all three, run around now in the carpeted room, play with toys and wrestle with each other and are starting to climb. They nurse whenever Emily has a mind to let them. She is still protective and solicitous, and loves just to lie and watch them at play. They sleep together most of the night.

June 3. They are eight weeks old today and ready for their first panleukopenia shot. As I examine each one as a show possibility, I decide that Little Emily has given me three excellent pets, but no Best in Show. They are clean, friendly, lovable, relaxed, playful and healthy—typical Pet Pride Kittens. The Greens from Santa Barbara want to buy White Satin and can hardly wait for him to join them. Of course, he cannot go until he has had his immunizing shot and is eating solid food. Since kittens are given immunization through the mother's milk, it is important that they be entirely weaned before given their shot. His two new prospective owners offer him a luxury home with constant human companionship. He will be neutered at nine months or even a little later if he doesn't start to spray. They want to change his name to Pasha.

Black Satin might turn into a good show cat. He has remarkable wide-apart round eyes. He will live with the Marquarts. They have eight other cats, all neuters and spays, who live happily with their two adults and one teenager, with the complete run of the house. Marlene in appearance is a little better than her mother but not as good-looking as her grand champion father. With her sweet lovely disposition she should be well loved all of her life. She was next to go. Hers was not a luxury home; she was taken by the delightful Jones family, complete with mother, father, sister, brother, and another cat, Black Shadow. She will have a wonderful life, I know.

Little Emily's Three had everything heredity and environment could give, plus love. As their owner, I offer a devout prayer that they will be well cared for always by their chosen Cat People.

Chapter 24

WHY NEUTER OR SPAY?

Rosalie Gordon of Good Shepard Foundation has expressed herself so well in this appeal to the public that I wish every casual cat owner could read it.

This is a plea on behalf of the unnumbered thousands of abandoned, unwanted animal waifs being born in our community. Cute and cuddly animals all of them, yet born under sentence of death, because there simply aren't and never could be that many homes.

Do you know that at this very moment untold thousands of surplus, unplaceable kittens and puppies are flooding and crowding and swarming their way into the world at a faster rate than they can be absorbed? A veritable deluge of kittens and puppies, but primarily kittens, in such fantastic, overwhelming numbers that fully 90% of them are foredoomed to suffering and premature death.

There is no computing the number that had their lives snuffed out in gas chambers during the past twelve months. Just a statistic in a public pound, yet each of these pathetic outcasts was a living, loyal creature, eager to shower its affection on some responsive human.

Still more thousands of innocent victims are doomed to

pay with their lives this year, guilty of no greater offense than that of being born in a world that has no place for them.

And all because some irresponsible pet owners have allowed their dogs or cats to roam at large, and breed, and add to the already enormous overpopulation of the animal world.

It has been mathematically estimated that one unspayed female can, in a period of ten years, increase the animal population by the staggering total of 84,652,644— assuming that all of them survived!

Are you guilty of contributing to this tragic picture by permitting your female pet to go unspayed? Stop this heartless, needless slaughter by spaying or altering your pet!

Contrary to popular belief, it is *not* best for an animal to be permitted to bear one litter. The widespread acceptance of this old wives' tale has caused incalculable mischief and suffering to the animal kingdom. Experience has shown that an altered pet makes a more satisfactory, sanitary and devoted pet in every way. A neutered male cat will not roam, fight, get into accidents, spray on furniture, or disturb the neighborhood by yowling in the wee hours of the morning. A good age at which to spay a puppy or kitten is five to six months. But any animal who is not too old to breed is not too old to spay.

If an accidental breeding has occurred, it is an act of mercy to put the litter to sleep at birth, immediately, before the consciousness of life has become firmly established. If you "haven't the heart" to put them out, you are only condemning them to a far unkinder fate later, and are directly responsible for the sufferings of a continuing army of unwanted offspring in the future. Such misguided tenderheartedness is neither merciful nor humane. It is responsible for a greater mass of animal misery than all forms of willful cruelty combined, since there will always be more animals than homes. Any veterinarian or humane society will administer euthanasia painlessly and advise you on drying up the mother's milk so she may be spayed.

Do not be deluded by the almost universal but mistaken belief that a nursing mother is immune against pregnancy. The fact is, when her kittens are barely two weeks old, she will almost surely set about preparing for her next litter— and so the whole weary round starts over again, until you decide to have her spayed.

A shocking number of irresponsible pet owners commit the callous crime of tossing out their unwanted kittens and puppies—or grown animals—abandoning them on highways, vacant lots or other people's property, on the possible assumption that someone else may be possessed of the kindness in which they themselves are lacking. If such persons could witness the fate that befalls these deserted animals—their bewilderment and panic, the hunted, wretched existence they lead, tortured by hunger and thirst, until they finally crawl off to starve and sicken and die—they could never rest easy again. The haunted expressions we have seen in the eyes of some of these animals would cure the most heartless of ever again seeking such a brutal solution to their problem.

Those who unrealistically oppose spaying on the grounds that it is "an interference with nature" or "a violation of an animal's right to procreate" fail to consider that the very existence of these animals is due to man's interference with nature. We bred these creatures and took them out of their native element where they had a chance to fend for themselves and nature herself maintained the balance. We placed them in the artificial environment of our civilization where they are absolutely dependent upon us. And when you consider that these little animals often start breeding when they are five or six months old, and can produce two or three litters a year, it requires no mathematician to realize that the surplus animal population soon reaches into astronomical figures. What alternative is there to spaying? Isn't prevention better than destruction?

In the face of these statistics, to permit your animal to bear a litter "because the children enjoy the puppies and kittens so" is a cruel and indefensible act. No living creature should be just a toy or plaything for a small child, though every youngster should be taught the love and proper care of pets. If you want the pleasure of a puppy or a kitten in your home and *are prepared to accept the responsibilities of pet ownership,* why not adopt some orphan from the public pound who would otherwise be marked for destruction? Don't be guilty of breeding more surplus animals to fall into irresponsible or abusive hands.

If you could follow up the fate of those puppies or kittens you "found good homes for"—and that of their offspring in turn—you would be appalled at the endless variety of tragedies that result from even a single instance of accidental breeding. We in humane work are daily confronted with these heartbreaking episodes, which run the gamut from starvation, freezing, accident and disease to the whole series of cruelties inflicted with intent by the callous and curious, each with its attendant train of misery and terror for the small helpless victims of surplus breeding.

To give away an unspayed female, especially, is to compound cruelty a thousandfold, and is the primary cause of the tragedies we are seeking to combat. It may be the very kitten you gave away that is responsible for that gaunt, emaciated mother cat foraging in garbage pails, her eyes haunted and harried in the losing struggle for survival for herself and her puny, frightened kittens.

Do your part this very day to eliminate this needless toll of suffering. The only solution lies in stopping the problem at its source by curtailment of breeding. We urge you to consult your veterinarian without delay in regard to spaying or altering your pet. If regular spaying fees are beyond your means, let us help you through our A-B-C (Animal Birth Control) Spaying Service. If you can afford to keep a pet, you can afford to spay it at our low rates.

If we are earnestly determined to improve conditions for all cats, we must intensify our work to awaken the public in general—make them conscious of the cats' sad plight in this world of ours.

Humane societies must do more than merely gather up the woeful and grievously distressed ones who through our unmindful negligence were allowed to be born in the first place.

Control of the population must be accomplished with neutering and spaying clinics, then our program of decent education on cat care must be implemented.

Here are some common questions asked about neutering and spaying:

Q: How often do female cats come into heat?

A: All female cats are different in this regard. Some females will come in season (heat) as often as every one or two weeks and go out of season between each heat for a varying number of days. Also, the age at which a female begins coming into season differs. In some cases, the female can begin as young as four months of age; others may be as much as a year old before their first season. Any cat who, in the course of the year, is almost constantly in season should be taken to the veterinarian for examination.

Q: Is it true that male cats that have not been neutered spray an unpleasant odor?

A: Yes, the spray of all male cats is very unpleasant. After the male has been neutered, he may still spray some, not as much as before, and the spray is much less pungent. The cat's natural physical makeup accounts for

the odor. It is nature's way of allowing the male cat to
mark off his territory and to announce his presence both
to other trespassing males as well as to females who wan-
der into his territory.

Q: Do cats who have been neutered or spayed develop
urinary stones and uretheral obstruction?

A: The problem of urinary blockage and stones is one
which is currently receiving extensive study by research
veterinarians. As of this writing, there have been no con-
clusive results which tie the onset of these problems to
any specific. Under consideration are diet, altering, a
virus, water content.

Q: Is it true that cats get lazy and fat after they have
been altered?

A: This is certainly not a truism. It is strictly a case of
proper diet and exercise. Any animal will become fat
and out of condition if improperly fed.

To reform the world for cats can only be done by
stamping out ignorance and concentrating on progressive
activities such as the development of charitable clinics,
ideal shelters, educational centers and helpful feline research. As this is being accomplished, attitudes toward the
cat will gradually change. We must through our literature
and our example encourage feelings of respect, love, ad-
miration for cats, and thus help to give them a better life.

Chapter 25

SUFFERING CATS!

If you think cats are not suffering in this world, give some quick attention to these: lost cats, lab cats, stray cats, caged cats, roaming cats, ill cats, shelter cats, casual-home cats and fighting cats.

Our cats are screaming for attention. Their appeal is obvious wherever we look. Are we ready to come to their rescue?

They are killed in the streets.

They are neglected in the home.

They are suffering in the laboratories.

They are being painfully declawed.

They are fed a malnourishing diet.

They are auctioned off at ten cents a pound to dealers.

They are poisoned by heartless people.

They are kept in small cages all of their lives.

They are breeding unwanted kittens.

They are covered with fleas, ear mites, fungus, and mats.

They are deprived of companionship.

They are ill for lack of medical attention.

They are allowed to get lost or stolen.

They are abandoned by the family who moves.

All of these cats are uncomfortable if not in actual pain. Those with worms are slowly dying of malnutrition. Some are weak from lack of food and water. Some with a

virus are about to die. Many have ear mites and are becoming deaf. Some have been run over and are dying by the roadside. Some are in laboratories and the anaesthesia is wearing off. Some are smarting with torn ears and lesions from fighting. Those being declawed are crying in pain. Some are bearing unwanted kittens in the weeds, under the house, or in the garage.

Some of these cats are being properly protected by their owners, responsible Cat People. Others have no owners. These suffering cats are in the majority. An estimated twenty million find their way into one of the euthanasia chambers of one of the humane societies every year. Most of these have already suffered in various ways. Only three hundred thousand cats have been registered during the last ten years. Of these, the majority are reasonably well cared for, compared to the stray cats. However, their homes also range from the poorest to the ideal. Many are caged without exercise and suffer a life of extreme boredom. Many of the caged cats are poorly groomed and poorly fed.

Although these cats are our responsibility, not enough of us are doing very much about them. Not many realize that the majority of our cats need help. Cats have been suffering in these ways for years. The number of suffering

cats will continue to grow unless steps are taken to halt the overbreeding of homeless cats and casual home cats.

People give many reasons for abandoning their cats. One of the commonest is moving to an apartment house where the manager (a Non-cat Person) allows no animals.

A new baby is sometimes the cause of the cat's becoming jealous and showing unpleasant personality traits. The owner can no longer be bothered to express love for the cat and for the baby at the same time. The owner cannot be patient and introduce the baby to the whole family, including the cat, as it is possible to do. So the cat is abandoned to his fate.

Sometimes a family will say, "We are going on vacation." And they leave the cat. Where is the sense of responsibility that a prospective owner should feel when he adopts a cat in the first place? A cat lives possibly fifteen years. A prospective owner should not adopt or buy a cat with the idea of "getting rid of the cat" in a few months or years for some flimsy reason—or no reason.

Many people, of course, try to find someone who will accept their cat. One reader wrote: "I am writing to you in the depths of despair, I need advice. My sister died suddenly of a heart attack and left a beloved cat who was the joy and light of her life. What does one do in such a case? The cat is a beautiful seven-year-old altered male. I cannot believe that removing him from life is moral and right. In this moment of bleak darkness I cannot see how I can take the cat with me, for I share a home with another teacher who has no liking for cats at all. To take my sister's beloved cat (and mine in a sense) into a situation like this seems unrealistic, for I am afraid that Alley P. Katz would be delegated to living in the cellar at best. He is used to love and my sister. He seems as lost as I without her. Yet there are six months of school before I could come home to the old house and Alley P. Katz. To leave him alone in the house to be fed by neighbors is cruel from the standpoint of his loneliness. To leave him indefinitely with one veterinarian or another does not seem very logical or good for him. What can people do in stiuations like this?"

Another reader wrote: "Am writing you for your good advice. There is a beautiful white cat in the yard of the apartment block where I live. I've found that he sleeps in accustomed discomfort in a sort of a dugout under the ground. I can't think how he manages to squeeze there. He is about two or three years old, obviously thrown out as a kitten, with signs of malnutrition. Otherwise he is in good condition, good coat, no ear mites or fleas. He first arrived about two months ago. He drew my attention one night as he was scrounging through the garbage can outside. I tossed him some food from our apartment window. He stayed around and I put food out for him. He had a haunted appearance and was terrified even to see me looking at him. Patient feeding has really tamed him and he now lets me pick him up. I made a weatherproof box

for him which he is using. He is a beautiful cat and most friendly to me. We can't have him because it wouldn't be fair to our own cat. I feel that a good home with someone who truly loves cats is what he deserves. He has been free too long, I think, to live in an apartment without a garden. I am most anxious to find him a home. I know the SPCA would only put him to sleep.

"Everyone wants adorable kittens. No one wants an older cat who has been through hell. Do you think I might be successful in advertising for a home? I hate to think of him out there with no one to love or properly care for him. I do as much as I can but he is still lonely under the present circumstances, and also we have a janitor who is quite capable of shooting him."

All cat associations and humane groups receive hundreds of letters a week with appeals such as this. Shelters, even if it were possible to build enough of them to house every homeless cat, are not the answer. The only real solution to this heartrending problem is education—education of every potential Cat Person in this country to the joys and responsibilities of cat ownership. Only then will people stop thinking that cats can take care of themselves. Only then will all cats be protected from the lives of suffering so many of them face today.

Oleta Smith of Texas makes a strong plea to Cat People who are keeping their cats in small cages. "We are all being made aware of the cruelty of caging cats. Many fanciers are joining us in trying to put a stop to this unspeakable thing. They will not sell cats or kittens to prospective buyers if the animals are destined to life inside a cage. The happy cat is the uncaged cat. Cats love to be free to run and play and curl up for a nap when tired.

"I have in mind a certain Himalayan. This cat was sold as a kitten in perfect health and was extremely playful, a round ball of fur with big, beautiful, blue eyes. The cat was from a popular, very much sought after bloodline. Now, just a year later, his owner is in despair because the cat is wasting away. Physically, he is in good health. The veterinarian can find nothing wrong with him. Why, then, is he down to skin and bones? The reason comes not from his breeding, as his owner thinks, but from a life too different from that which he knew as a kitten. Confined in a cage, away from human companionship, this poor unfortunate cat will live out his days and die in loneliness. This is just one case. There are thousands more the world over."

Some cats are declawed by their owners. This puts the

cat in an unshowable class and is in most cases a great handicap from the cat's point of view. Study these drawings of the bones of the feet.

Note the strong ligaments and tendons which give power to extend and retract the claws. This is unique in your cat. Without this he cannot grasp, hold, or establish footing for walking, running, springing, climbing, or stretching. When the end digit, including the claw, is removed, the sensory and motor nerves are cut, damaged and destroyed. They do not repair themselves or grow back for many months. There follows a wooden lack of feeling, then a tingling sensation during the long convalescence. The cat must walk on the stub end of the second digit.

Since cats have keener senses than humans, they suffer

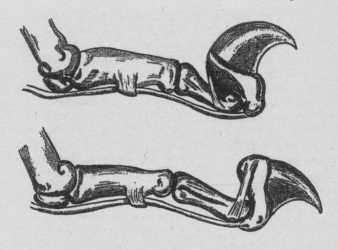

more than we do. Many pain-killing drugs, including aspirins, do not agree with cats and can cause illness or death. Anyone who has undergone bone surgery will appreciate the problem that can be created by the inability to medicate for pain.

There are many instances of the claws growing back, but not in the normal way; rather, they grow up through the top of the paw, creating a bloody sore.

The cat's whole body is especially well designed. The skeleton is more elastic and better jointed than that of the dog. In the shoulder there is so much play that the shoulder blade may touch the jaw or slide back as far as the eighth or tenth rib. All muscles governing this lithe little body are highly developed. This naturally gives the cat great climbing power (if he is not deliberately handicapped by a human).

The sharp claws that can be whipped out for business or tucked neatly away are fanciest of all. The elastic tendon holds the claw in its own sheath. The claw is flat on each side the better to slide in and out. When the cat pulls his claw down with the use of the big tendon that lies along the under part of the toe, the ligament stretches like a fresh rubber band. It is hooked on the end for hanging on. Cats like to keep their claws sharp and clean by working on the scratching post you provide.

Besides the physical mutilation, consider what this operation may do to the cat's emotions and the personality changes that may occur. One woman we know sold her cat and found later that the new owner had the cat declawed. The cat had gone berserk. Since he had no claws to defend himself, he constantly growled and wanted to bite everyone who came near. His disposition was completely changed. The cat was returned to the original owner, who had to keep him caged. Finally, since he could not adjust to clawless life, he had to be euthanized.

If you really love your cat and want him to live a pleasant long life with you, it is safer to protect him from this kind of suffering.

The drawings of the retracted and extended claws and the bones of the foot were done by artist El Jon.

WARDS (Welfare of Animals used in Research for Drugs and Surgery) claims that most people don't believe that pets are stolen. Why would anyone do that? they ask. They know that purses are snatched, but surely not pets. But the market for pets for research is profitable, and the well-cared-for, friendly family pet is an easy prey. To prevent pet napping, never leave your animal alone even in your own yard. Lock your car when your pet is in it. In hot weather when this is not possible, keep your pet at home.

When your animal is stolen, the thief usually gives it a massive dose of sleeping medicine and it is piled in with others. Those who live often go to "dealers" where they are kept under filthy conditions and starved. Here the best are sold for better prices. Finally, half dead and cowed, your pet is taken to an auction or trade day where its source is seldom recorded. From here it lands in a labora-

tory. As it changes hands everyone gets his cut so long as the poor creature can stand up.

When the 89th Congress, by an overwhelming majority, passed Public Law 89-544, the Laboratory Animal Welfare Act, in August, 1966, the humanitarians might well have supposed that relief from the intolerable conditions of dealers' premises, animals in transit, and in research laboratories, was in sight. However, opposition behind the scenes began its work almost immediately. When the Congress passed the law that established Federal standards for the care of animals used in medical research, it provided for inspection and enforcement by the appropriate agency, the Animal Health Division of the Department of Agriculture. This division has a large staff of veterinarians with a splendid record for eradicating disease among farm animals and also has a corps of inspectors experienced in enforcement work.

The opposition wants to wreck the existing law by the simple device of shifting the inspection of laboratories and research centers from the Department of Agriculture to the Department of Health, Education, and Welfare. HEW has no existing staff to handle this assignment. Most humanitarians feel that Congress should leave well enough alone. All the Department of Agriculture needs to proceed with enforcement of the law is a more adequate appropriation.

Humanitarians are only interested in cutting to a minimum the sufferings of laboratory animals. This means using fewer animals, housing them comfortably (not in small cages with wire mesh flooring), and using anaesthesia when painful experiments are performed.

Suffering cats—they can be found in many places. But not enough people recognize them, or spend much time thinking about them. If they do begin to have insight into the problems of the vast millions of miserable cats, they are quick to turn away with the excuse that they can't stand it. Those of us who are willing to accept this burden of understanding can do so by becoming involved in varying activities that lead to insuring a comfortable life for all cats.

Part III

THE WORLD
OF CATS

Chapter 26

DRUCILLA—THE CAT OF
MANY COLORS

"A little cat played on a silver flute
  And a big cat sat and listened;
The little cat's strains gave the big cat pains
  And a tear on his eyelids glistened."

Arthur Macy (1842-1904)

She isn't a calico, or a tortie, or a bluecream. She's nothing but a Cat of Many Colors. She was dumped at the shelter by a woman who bothered with no show of sympathy. The kitten had been making a nuisance of itself yowling at her back door. Every time the door was opened, this pest tried to enter the house.

I was asked if I'd take the kitten for a time to give her the care she needed. My answer was, "Yes—just give her her shots and hurry over."

To give the waif a feeling of belonging, we gave her a name: Drucilla. When Drucilla was brought out of her carrier, she was a scrawny parcel of dirty kitten, on the verge of malnutrition. But she wasn't beaten.

The problem of fleas and dirt came first—next was her constant diarrhea.

Through lack either of strength or mother cat training, she paid no attention to the soiling she caused. Washing and drying her little rump was no small task. She would have none of this indignity! Where in that frail body of hers was all that resistance hidden? The cleanup job finally worked itself into a frenzy and became a match between her hidden strength and mine.

Melts are a good food with which to combat malnutrition. I tried them on her. No go. My next try was to scrape the melts to mix with other foods. Ever try scraping a piece of slimy, bloody meat? When the job was done, my kitchen looked like an abattoir, and I like a victim.

Mother Nature must have whispered, "It's up to you—take over." Drucilla did. Her food and shots were assimilated by her starved body. And as her body was nourished, her many colors were brought into play.

Her coat has the brilliant red of the smoke cameo, the even lavender-blue shade of the Russian Blue, the heavy silver sheen of the Korat, the warm sable of the Burmese, the color variations of the Siamese, plus the rich, mahogany brown of the Havana. All these colors of different breeds are splayed over the underlying color of the chinchilla.

Impossible to combine into one clear, beautiful blend? Not to Mother Nature. She is the supreme artist in handling the magnitude—the vibrations—of the whole spectrum.

When Drucilla uncurls, gives the S stretch that all cat lovers enjoy, then faces one, the effect is startling.

Two ears, transparently thin, are alerted into a keen perk (she sleeps with them alert). One ear has a cast of

shaded silver abruptly finished into pink at the base. The
other ear is slashed in two parts of color: one with the
same base of the silver but intermixed with all her other
colors; the other half is pink.

To some, Drucilla has a prissy sound. But this growing
kitten proves the Latin meaning, "strong." And her eyes
portray the Greek meaning, "dewey-eyed."

Those eyes of hers bring forth a sign of wonder. In the
poor health of her babyhood they were murky and brown-
yellow. Now they are pieces of burnished bronze, high-
lighted by the sun.

Her nose has not decided what pattern it's going to
follow. However, it definitely has nostrils in two shades,
one a pure cherry pink, the other pink brushed with
bluish-brown. When they quiver or twitch, the resultant
pattern is hard to follow.

The fur of her nose is like damp velvet. The built-in
dolphin smile of her mouth is cherub pink.

Her white fluff, or collar, is not the Elizabethan type
worn by many cats, but a soft, short, downy cape. A thin
brown strip zags through the bottom edge, which gives a
rakish appearance, as if her cape had gone a bit askew.

When she rolls over, either to look at the ceiling or for
a quick nap, her belly shows a refined white. When she's
in this position I sometimes see a dusting of lustrous
black. But on closer inspection, the marks are not to be
found. If I try to rub the hairs of her belly in different
lines and swirls, the phenomenon hides. Are dark colors
lying at the roots of the hairs, waiting to come up and
break through?

The side views of her body are exciting in brilliant
light. Both sides have a whirlpool pattern made of bands
of her dominant colors, separated by a lacy fringe of
silver. The whorls end with rings down her legs, in a
mixture of all her colors.

On her front legs, these tabby markings come to an

abrupt stop one-half inch from the toes proper, which are a free white. Her back legs carry the tabby rings down to the first hind joint. The exceptionally long legs from there on are softer white. This part of her hind legs suggests Siamese to some. When she was a starved babe, she looked like a wizened kitten on the legs of a kangaroo.

Three of her pads are a flush pink—one back pad is daubed in color as is her one nostril.

Drucilla has the normal kitten's meow, but in rough play, or when calling to me or the other cat for special attention, the call has the tone of an adult Siamese. It varies from a low-running trill to a dolorous meauoo, and sometimes hits a crescendo of demanding "You-owe-MEE!"

To Drucilla, her tail is a toy. Where the elusive thing comes from—where it disappears—is the game of games for her, and for others who watch. In her hunt for it, she goes into complete somersaults. Her coming to a short stop—thinking to outwit this skillful knave—is a one-act comedy. When she's at this trick in the bathtub, it's pure slapstick.

She seems to choose two A.M. for another number in her extensive repertoire. Her entrance bit is usually that of routing Wfyah, my other cat, out of a sleep. A boxing and combined wrestling match then follows. The resulting thump of their two bodies on the hollow-sounding floor not only awakens me but puts me into a fit of anxiety. Will the people in the apartment below complain?

Not all Drucilla's healthy growth is due to diet. The cat Wfyah—who also was once a waif—has taken over Drucilla's education in the ways and means of battle. Drucilla has mastered isometrics and isotonics, and is currently learning judo. I suppose karate will be next.

I use a rubber-bladed fan in my workroom. The rubber blades are for safeguarding the noses of nosey cats. One day while in another room, I heard an irregular low-toned thump and whine coming from the workroom. I rushed in. I should have known. Drucilla was putting one front paw, then the other, against the blades. She seemed to like the feeling. The rubber blades won't slash or cut, yet they can give even heavy-skinned fingers a sensation that's not pleasant. Drucilla's tastes and whims are as varied as her colors.

When Wfyah followed me and saw what I saw, she went into shock. It took me over a day and a night to wheedle her into the workroom again.

Now that Drucilla is finally slowing down a little, I should be relieved. But instead I sometimes wish her again to be a small, spooky, mischief-making kitten.

Her devilment is not from the meanness we humans sometimes yield to. Her witchery is the fun of growing up.

I have a belief that cats help us understand how much we need to be loved and how to deserve that love.

Drucilla—the Cat of Many Colors—with the bits in her of the cat world's finest, is working hard at firming my belief.

Dit Colee

Chapter 27

THE SHOW MANAGER HAS AN EXCITING WEEKEND!

Four o'clock Saturday morning—not too early to wake up and get the cats ready for their carriers. They are bathed, their nails are clipped, their teeth are cleaned and they are thoroughly groomed. For months before—in fact, for all of their lives—they have had excellent care: wholesome diet, companionship, exercise and play. All three are amenable, easy to handle, pleasant with strangers. They will never hurt any judge.

We arrive at the show hall at six and stand in a short line with the others. All five veterinarians are on the job. Five girls in uniform are acting as assistants. The tables are thoroughly sterilized between each exhibitor's cats. All five hundred cats look well as they are checked in. No cats have to be turned down for not being clean or in good health.

At nine o'clock we must be ready to start. This will be a strenuous three-hour period: checking in; giving out exhibitors' cards with the cats' numbers; having exhibitors find their cages, put up their cage curtains, decorate their grooming spaces; store their traveling equipment under the tables. I will be looking at the new catalog and taking care of last-minute information on absentees and transfers.

The exhibitors are friendly and polite to me—the show manager. So far everyone seems to be complying with the requests I made in the confirmation letter I sent out this year. I review the letter in my mind as I greet each new exhibitor:

Welcome to our Show. We are looking forward with great anticipation to your safe arrival with all of your Cats. Remember the time—we start at nine on Saturday. On Sunday be there at 8:15—to get your Cat and his cage ready for the day. Clean water. Clean litter. Keep things off the tops of the cages. Keep your grooming space neat and presentable for the sake of the public and our reputation. Certain requests we made last year helped to make ours a quality Show. May we ask you again for the sake of our Cats to be *composed* and *friendly* and help us to:

1. MAKE A GOOD IMPRESSION ON THE GENERAL PUBLIC as Cat Fanciers and as Cat owners. They will like the Cats more if they like the people who own them. Remember, for two days you and your Cats are "on stage." The well-dressed, well-groomed Exhibitor helps make our Cats important.
2. KEEP THE SHOWROOM NEAT AND CLEAN. For your convenience we will provide ash trays and large brown paper bags. Place all used litter in the brown paper bags and leave near trash containers at the end of the Show. We cannot leave litter all over the floor.

3. KEEP THE SHOW RUNNING SMOOTHLY AND ON SCHEDULE. Check-in hours are 6:15 A.M. until 8:45 A.M. Be ready to exhibit at 9 A.M. when judging begins. We wish to use the microphone as little as possible in order to keep a quiet show room. Watch for your numbers and bring your Cats to the Judge's cage promptly. Cooperate with our Master of Ceremonies.

4. WELCOME THE OUT-OF-TOWNERS. Many are coming from long distances. We want them to know we are friendly and hospitable. They will be anxious to meet you, so look them up in our catalog and introduce yourself. The First-Timers will appreciate any help you can give them; remember when?

5. BE PLEASANT TO OUR VISITORS. They are interested in Cats or they wouldn't be with us. Many are future Fanciers and prospective customers for your kittens, and they all want to know about Cats. If you are busy when they speak to you, please excuse yourself pleasantly and ask them to return when you'll have the opportunity to talk with them.

6. PROTECT YOUR CAT DURING THE SHOW. Ask your neighbor to keep an eye on him if you have to leave your cage area and offer to do the same for his Cats when he leaves. Be alert to your Cat's behavior in the judging ring. Be ready *instantly* to take over if called. No Cats should be left in the Show Room overnight. This practice is very boring to the Cats and *unsafe*. They need companionship and attention after a day at the Show. If found in the auditorium after hours Saturday

night, Cats will be removed to a boarding home.

7. MAKE CATS POPULAR. The care and devotion you show your Cat may make others more Cat-conscious and help our objective—more humane treatment of all Cats. A cherished, appreciated Cat is his own best publicity agent. Always remember to handle your Cat in public as if you were teaching a novice the correct and proper way.

8. CONTROL YOUR CHILDREN. We love to have children at the Show but they also may have only "controlled freedom" as do our Cats. We cannot allow them to play and run in the lobby or auditorium or balcony seats. This disturbs the Visitors, Exhibitors, Cats and Judges. None of the Members has time to discipline and control small children, much as we would love to. This is the responsibility of the parents. The children must be accompanied at all times by an adult and held by the hand if necessary.

Our sincere thanks to you for all that you do to make our Show a success. Thank you very much for your loyal support.

I notice how the Household Pet people are benched among the old-time exhibitors, and are being initiated into the ways of show people. I see one reading her Bulletin entitled, "Why not enter your household pet?" This is what she is learning:

One of the most popular shows within a Show is for Household Pets. This Show is made up of mixed-breed cats who are fascinating in appearance, each different from any other cat in the world, all groomed to perfection, all healthy, clean and friendly. These

Pets have had a great share of their owner's companionship.

You, the Household Pet Owners, check in Saturday morning with the Veterinarian. You settle down among the owners of the championship classes and prepare for two full days of enjoyment and cat education. Naturally you have prepared your cat for the show some weeks in advance, by being sure each day he is clean, healthy, well brushed and combed. Within a week of the show a good soap and water bath is a necessity. His teeth and ears should be checked. His nails clipped—only the tips. The Veterinarian will examine him closely. He should be in top physical condition with no ear mites, fleas or skin trouble of any kind. If he is not a clean, healthy, strong cat, he will be disqualified by the Veterinarian who will examine all cats before the show starts on Saturday. Only clean, healthy cats will be allowed in the Show Hall.

When getting ready for the great event, you should prepare some simple, or better still, fancy curtains to hang inside your show cage. Any good quality, solid colored fabric (silk, satin, nylon, cotton, velvet) can be used (solid to match your cat's eyes or coat usually, not always, shows off your cat to better advantage, than spotted, striped, or plaid backgrounds) either gathered on the top, or French pleated, or arranged to lie smooth against the *inside* of the cage. Don't throw a towel around the outside of your cage and call it dressed. Also, bring a yard of good fancy ruglike material for the floor of the cage, thick enough to lie flat. Plan to have another yard of fancy material to place smooth and flat on top of the cage. This should match or harmonize with curtains inside the cage.

Don't forget to bring a small, neat litter tray and your cat's best water and food dishes. Some Fanciers place a small decorative screen in front of the litter pan for cat privacy. Others provide fancy little beds. Bring your cat into the Show Hall in an attractive, neat cat carrier (not an old, rusty, makeshift beaten-up box) preferably with a well-made tailored fabric cover for protection. Your cat will be happier and less scared if he enters the Show Hall in a carrier he is used to and it is covered. There are always prizes for the best decorated cage. You are proud of your Cat. You now are becoming a part of the Fancy—and want to make a good impression (as to your own dress and behavior in public).

You will have time before your Cat comes up for judging to watch the other Exhibitors and see what they do. Watch the Judge quietly and patiently. Watch for your number to be called. Place your Cat in the Judge's cage quickly and as unobtrusively as possible. The Judge doesn't wish to know whose Cat belongs to whom. You can help keep this a secret. Do not ever speak to the Judge until the whole show is entirely over. Give the Judge time to figure out his finals in solemn concentration. Do not call attention to your entry while he is being judged. Do not interrupt the Judge to take pictures or ask questions. In fact, *do not talk at all* while watching the judging, expecially if you are sitting near the front of the audience. A cat show should always be reasonably quiet. Cats don't like noise, except their own, and can be seriously disturbed. . . .

What will you win?—possibly Best Household Pet, Most Interestingly Marked Cat, Best Dispositioned Cat, Smartest Cat, Best Groomed Cat, Greatest Actor, Healthiest Cat, Brightest Colored Cat, Best Show-Off Cat, Most Lovable Cat, or the Most Unusual Cat.

If you like Cats, consider one of the most exciting, wholesome, and popular hobbies in these United

States and Canada. This is the hobby that is not only fun to be in, *it does more humane work* for the Cat than any other activity in our country. Why not be a part of our great work for Cats by entering YOUR Household Pet?

Nine o'clock comes all too quickly. The master of ceremonies is in his place at the podium with the loudspeaker. The judges' rings are set up around the edges of the two far sides of the room. They are all seen at a glance by the visitors as they enter. The exhibitors can watch all the rings at once if need be. The cats' numbers on the judges' cages are large and I can see them across the room. The exhibitors are grooming their cats to perfection with a final brush. They are arranging their decorations and settling down to watch. The judges, clerks, and stewards are all in their places. It is 8:30 A. M. The clerks are putting their ribbons in order. They are checking the absentees and transfers.

The master clerk is surveying the whole situation with pride. The stewards know their instructions and are sitting quietly at one side of their rings. The master of ceremonies is introducing the judges. The show is starting. Each judge is beginning his day of handling one hundred fifty cats. This task is not an easy one and takes a highly qualified and professionally trained person. There are probably not more than one hundred highly trained judges in the United States and Canada today.

The show progresses excitingly and quietly with a high degree of suspense. The visitors begin to pour in. As they look at each decorated cage, all with their beautiful purebreds and unusual mixed-breeds, I hear my members talking with them. I am pleased they are promoting in every way possible the objectives of our Cat Fanciers Association club:

1. To encourage breeding to standard of both long-haired and shorthaired cats.
2. To hold shows and promote interest in and knowledge of cats.
3. To cultivate sentiments of friendship and common interest among members.
4. To advance in every possible way the interests of fanciers, exhibitors, and pet owners.
5. To promote cats and kittens as clean, healthy, delightful pets.
6. To encourage the neutering and spaying of all cats not to be used in selective breeding.
7. To urge the layman to protect all cats from disease and exploitation.
8. To make cat shows, conventions, exhibitions, seminars, cat clubs, and study groups interesting and popular.
9. To raise money for the less fortunate cats.
10. To make an annual contribution to support the region as a whole.
11. To cooperate with and offer financial aid to other CFA clubs in the area when needed.

Now it is Saturday afternoon. There is a long waiting line in front of the box office. Once in, the visitors are fascinated with the lobby exhibits. Cat things galore are on display: cat furniture; cat toys; cat art; cat food; cat jewelry; cat food supplements; cat books; cat magazines; cat stationery; and cat grooming equipment. The various humane societies, including Mercy Crusade, Pet Assistance Foundation and some shelter cats, each have been given important space. The Cat People are intrigued with all these cat things and patronize the promoters for the sake of their cats at home. Some of the larger Pet Pride approved companies have costly displays which include colored movies of other shows.

Twenty clean, healthy, bathed shelter cats are set up in

special displays with identical curtains, water dishes and litter trays. I see their sign—Love for Sale. The form and contract signed by an adopter is being filled in by a prospect. These are the comments and questions he is reading on the Adopter's Form:

> We are deeply concerned with the kinds of homes our cats go into and the attitudes of their owners toward them. Will you kindly answer the following questions:
>
> 1. Are you willing to keep your cat in your home at all times unless out on leash, in a carrier, or in a safe, screened area?
> 2. Will you provide your cat with a clean litter tray daily?
> 3. If your cat is not already spayed or neutered, are you willing to have this done at the age of eight months?
> 4. Will you make every effort to keep your cat clean, free of all parasites, and give him medical attention when necessary?
> 5. May we telephone you or visit with you within a reasonable length of time to see how your cat is adjusting to your home?
> 6. How many hours of companionship can you give your cat a day?
> 7. Will your cat have other animal company besides his human companionship?
>
> All kittens and cats in the shelter have had their protective shots, are clean and free of ear mites, worms, fungus, or fleas. All adult cats have been neutered or spayed.

I see that he has now finished filling in the form. He is taking Sparky in cage 19. He is being presented with a package of litter, a new plastic litter tray, a cat care manual and a new cardboard carrier.

It is now 7 P.M. The first day's Show is drawing to a close. The exhibitors are taking all cats out of the Show Room for the night. Where? To a hotel room possibly. Cats must have relief from a show cage. They must exercise and have food and rest in preparation for the Sunday show.

Sunday is here. Another exciting day! The judges are on duty. The clerks are putting up the first sets of numbers. Everyone is looking rested and enthusiastic. Now we are beginning to know who will be in the Final Best of the Best ceremony. The Show Hall is becoming so crowded the exhibitor can hardly get his cat up to the judge's cage. Fortunately, the area is air-conditioned for cats' comfort and health. The friendly, eager crowd presses forward, forgetting what it means for the exhibitor to reach his judging cage on time. As the exhibitor tries politely to weave his way to his ring, he is stopped with oh's and ah's—what a beautiful cat! The exhibitor is pleased. Any other time he would take all kinds of time to explain the wonders of his cat. But timing is all important here if the show is to meet its deadline. The deadline must not be later than 8 P.M., this Sunday night—preferably sooner.

The show is moving at a fast clip! A peak time for visitors—at two o'clock on Sunday afternoon the second Household Pet Show is being staged. There are sixty entries.

I watch the judging with great interest. Drucilla, my Cat of Many Colors, is acting like an angel. Just out of her kitten stage, she is an ideal example of what can be done with a stray mixed-breed. She looks beautiful! Someone tells me Drucilla is the prettiest cat she has ever seen. For my part, of course, she always takes my breath away when I suddenly come upon her. Her fur, patched, spotted and striped, has a sheen all its own.

The Third Best is chosen. The Second Best is chosen. The large audience is quiet, alert and intent. Who will be

chosen Best Household Pet? The judge walks up and
down the row of cages once more—pretending this time
not even to glance Drucilla's way. Then—he walks
straight to her cage—he picks her up, he holds her high!
Drucilla is BEST CAT!

What a triumph! Drucilla, my poor stray, sickly, for-
lorn, mixed-breed shelter kitten—rescued—given the best
of care. How she is rewarding me! Perhaps this will
answer those uninformed people who are always trying to
tell us cat fanciers that we "don't love stray cats."

The last of the regular judging is being finished. We
know now who the twenty-four finalists will be. Finally,
the Best Of The Bests is chosen by the highly qualified,
experienced referee judge. Twenty-four Best Cats from
each of the shows are lined up side by side. They rep-
resent a cat from every breed. Here is a group of cats
who are truly representative of the finest cats in the world.

Each cat is carried by the judge to her table. Each cat is
examined thoroughly and carried back to the judge's cage.
While all twenty-four cats are judged, the quiet, intense
audience watches intently. The referee judge's peers, fellow judges, are sitting on the front seats. Each of them
wonders if the referee is going to choose his "Best Cat."

Finally, the Fifth Best Cat is selected. Then the Fourth
Best is selected—the Third Best—the Second Best—and
—with great applause—now, the BEST OF THE BEST!
He wins the Felix Award, which the owner accepts with
pride.

And so the grande finale ends now with pictures and
congratulations and tears of joy. The little fellow who won
is purring contentedly in his owner's arms.

Chapter 28

OUR GREATEST HOPE—A GOOD FUTURE FOR ALL CATS!

"But thousands die without this or that,
    Die, and endow a college or a cat."
                              Alexander Pope (1688-1744)

We estimate that one-fourth of the people in these United States—some fifty million—think enough of cats potentially to direct their attention to some particular pet. Fifty million potential Cat People are enough for us to unify. Let us direct our intellectual effort aggressively toward this group.

Only in the last few years in our country has the cat been singled out among small animals as an individual who is different in his needs, preferences and rights from other animals. His diet and his health, the kinds of protection he needs, the quality of environment he must have, the type of companionship he enjoys—these are all peculiar to the cat. The diseases he is subject to are as numerous as those of the human and many of them are similar. The degree of his intelligence and understanding we can only guess.

Some people think that if we humans were wiser we would have a more mystical concept of animals. Remote as we are from nature and its beauty, we tend to patronize animals for their incompleteness and to think of them as being far below ourselves. How often someone comes forth with, "He acts just like an animal!" This is not intended as a compliment to the animal. Yet the animal world is older and saner than ours. The animals' senses are keener than ours. For all we know, they are hearing voices we will never hear.

Joy Adamson, the author of *Born Free,* shows us the great importance of the man-animal relationship. She writes: "Man cannot separate himself from the rest of his fellow creatures. Ecology means the cooperation of every living thing. We invent our own destruction."

This attitude helps us develop a respect for our animal, appreciation of him and understanding of his position in our lives. If we are to stand behind the cat to overcome his problems for him and gain recognition and respect for him, a vast program of promotion is necessary. In this promotion the cat himself is our greatest asset; both as a show cat and as a cared-for household pet. We know that millions upon millions of stray mixed-breed homeless cats have lives too harassed and confused to be worth living. These are the cats who must be brought into the household pet class. Their population must be controlled with money properly spent by a humane-minded organization, one which understands the project and how to execute it.

We are gathering our resources in order to rescue, in countless neighborhoods in the United States and Canada, the starving, sick, abused and maligned cats. We must teach the careless owner how to care for his household pet, and we must protect the purebred cat from being exploited—or becoming extinct. All cats should live in an environment that is at least comfortable. If buyers of kittens deal with a highly recommended person, the serious problem of exchanging kittens will be solved. Increasing the number of well-cared-for cats—as against the number of sadly neglected cats—is an important part of our program.

Resources will not be forthcoming from any public fund since our government is overwhelmed with human problems. Since no thought will probably be given to the needs of our animals, and since nothing can be done for cats without money, their benefactors will have to be discovered. Who will they be—the private generous individual, the corporation blessed with thinking leaders, or the great mass of concerned people, Cat People, each giving what he can? Possibly a combination of all three will be the answer.

Money is needed first. A great deal of money. Think what this cleanup operation will cost! We must get cats from under houses, out of the weeds, away from the woodpile, away from garages and basements. And along with mass population control we must continue to teach good common basic truths of proper cat care.

Little has ever been spent on our cats for their own sakes. Millions are spent every year by the Department of Health, Education, and Welfare *on* cats but not *for* cats. Large grants by the million are given to the laboratories to spend on the purchase of stray household pets from "licensed dealers." Then other large sums are given to the research person so that he may discover—possibly for the hundredth time—some scientific secret from the live bodies of our little cats.

With humane scientific research *for the benefit of the cat,* we are wholly in accord. Some of our oldest and largest humane societies spend millions every year on euthanasia alone. They spend little, if anything, on the prevention of breeding. These particular millions could well be spent on education of the public on the proper care of cats. Neutering and spaying would make euthanasia unnecessary.

We must acquire funds to start cat educational centers, clinics and shelters across the country to change this world for them and make living in it at least acceptable. Every community under our guidance—and with our money—could begin this huge task of befriending homeless cats.

If we can build a cat center in every state, our cat will be, generally speaking, on his way to a better environment, more popular and in better health. Our Fancy will be more affluent, more exciting, more influential. Our humane workers will be less harassed and less frustrated over the plight of the less fortunate cat.

If at first euthanasia of some half-wild cats is found necessary, a neutering and spaying program will lessen the number as work is carried on. The important thing is to start the program and make the pendulum swing toward a lesser population of homeless cats each year, not a greater one.

We must simultaneously develop our model Cat Town. The most important asset of this town must be the world-famous Pet Pride Park located on a few acres within the boundaries of the town. Will this be a second Disneyland —promoting cats only? It could be.

The cat has lived for years as a second-class animal citizen. He has been misunderstood, maligned and unappreciated. It behooves Cat People to present the cat to the public as an animal truly deserving of consideration. The more the layman learns about the cat—about his needs, personality, companionable characteristics—the better the cat will fare. The more the managers of apartment houses learn about cats, the more opportunities cats will have for good homes. Cooperation and understanding here would increase the cat-owning population by the millions. Establishment of a Cat Town would do much to publicize the needs of cats.

Cat Town will surround the Park with its hotels, apartment houses, shopping centers, residential areas and industrial areas for the manufacture of cat items. Let us pray that this town will be beautiful and that it will be well planned with underground utilities. The Park itself will include a hall to accommodate five hundred cats for

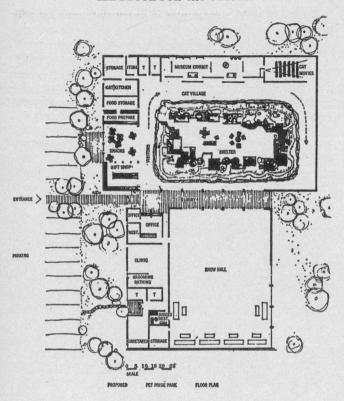

PROPOSED   PET PRIDE PARK   FLOOR PLAN

routine shows. It will also include a clinic with modern
grooming and bathing facilities, a lobby with our museum
and Hall of Fame. Of course, it will include the cat snack
bar and gift shop.

Adjoining and connected with the hall, the most beautiful shelter ever conceived is being planned. The shelter
will include a series of chalets for colony living with
hundreds of feet of continuous runs. These should be
enjoyed by all shelter cats. Visitors may view the cats

through the glass wall surrounding the chalets. The very decorative concept of the shelter is unique, glamorous and inspiring. It will add tremendous interest to an already developing American hobby. It could even inspire visitors to donate to the cause of less fortunate cats.

The first Cat Town may be located in California—the home base of Pet Pride. State Executive Field Directors, however, will be promoting Cat Centers in other parts the United States and Canada. The acreage to be developed should be large enough for surrounding expansion. Food corporations will want to have permanent displays as will food supplement companies and laboratories. One national registering body, the largest one, will possibly relocate. Feline research will be carried on to benefit the cat's health. The town will become the center for the manufacture of cat products.

Pet Pride sees a great future for cats. This future will come to pass because of the imagination, the enthusiasm and the dedication of all Pet Pride's members and friends —they who dearly love cats!

INDEX

191

**VICTORIAN,
THE CINDERELLA OF ANTIQUES**   Carl W. Drepperd
The information covers tables, beds, mirrors, jewelry, china and
much more. Fully illustrated!   A681—95¢

WINNING DECLARER PLAY   Dorothy Hayden
A top bridge player describes the play in an easy-to-follow way.
Each chapter contains sample hands to enable you to test your
understanding.   A620—$1.25

HOME WINEMAKER'S HANDBOOK
                    Walter S. Taylor and Richard P. Vine
A detailed, step-by-step guide to making wines of all types—
dinner wines, dessert wines, champagne, and more—in your own
home . . . *easily and inexpensively!*   A684—95¢

THE WEDDING BOOK   Frances and Frederic A. Birmingham
A most unique wedding guide—*with complete information for
both bride and groom*—that tells you what to do and explains
in detail exactly how to do it.   A761—95¢